Proper
Telly

Also available by Stuart Ball

Trotter Trivia: The Only Fools & Horses Quiz Book

The Great British Sitcom Quiz Book

80s Quiz Master

A Question of Carry On

Proper Telly

Stuart Ball

Published by Kindle Direct Publishing
Cover image: Parinki/Shutterstock

First published 2018

ISBN-13: 978-1729492222

This one is for Lisa, my inspiration and continual source of happiness.

Contents

WANDRIN' STAR – PROPER TELLY BIRTHDAYS

At 7:15pm on Thursday 19 March 1970, Tony Blackburn was the presenter of the latest edition of *Top of the Pops* on BBC1. The official UK Top 40 singles chart on this day was awash with legends from all areas of the musical spectrum. Old school crooners such as Jim Reeves, Andy Williams and Frank Sinatra were jostling for chart positions alongside new acts The Jackson Five and Brotherhood of Man. Elvis Presley was sitting inside the Top 10 with *Don't Cry Daddy* while The Beatles were enjoying their swansong with *Let It Be*.

Somewhat incongruously however, the coveted number one slot on the UK chart that day was not held by any of these greats of the music scene. Instead, that honour went to a grizzled Hollywood veteran who sang like he had just gargled with a handful of rusty nails and then smoothed over the resulting abrasions with sand paper. That man was Lee Marvin.

The musical western *Paint Your Wagon,* in which Marvin had co-starred with Clint Eastwood, had recently been a huge hit in cinemas on both sides of the Atlantic. Although the film's musical score, first penned by Alan J Lerner and Frederick Loewe for the stage in 1951, included such strangely hypnotic gems as tough guy Clint warbling *I Talk to the Trees,* it was Lee Marvin's melancholy rough-hewn vocal rendition of *Wand'rin Star* which really captured the public's attention.

Released as a single on February 7 1970, *Wandr'in Star* hit the top spot on March 7 and stayed there for three weeks, holding off the challenge of The Beatles, who had to be satisfied with a high of number 2 for their farewell single.

As Tony Blackburn introduced another dance routine from the divine Pan's People, fond memories of whom still linger in the minds of all seventies dads, a young mum was attending to her newly born second child. That child was me.

I love the fact that Lee Marvin was at number one on the day I first came into the world. As far as I am concerned, I truly was born under a wandr'in star. It is an excellent song to have as the number one single on the day you were born. Certainly when you compare it to a long-time friend of mine. He made his first appearance in life to the off-kilter bellowing of the England World Cup Squad with *Back Home*. Poor chap.

In addition to the aforementioned *Top of the Pops*, the BBC1 schedule on the day I was born included such wonderful delights as *Tom and Jerry, The Flowerpot Men* and *The Basil Brush Show;* the rather well-spoken fox introducing Herman's Hermits as his special guests that week. Later that evening, the BBC's legendary sports anchor David Coleman presented the latest edition of *Sportsnight,* which featured highlights from the World Ice Hockey Championships from Sweden and analysis of the previous night's European football. Meanwhile, over on BBC2, Robert Robinson was chairing another edition of the gloriously cosy *Call My Bluff.*

In the course of researching *Proper Telly*, I have delved into the vast archives of the British Broadcasting Corporation to see what other gems were screened on later birthdays. When I turned five in 1975, the big film on BBC1 that evening was *The Brides of Fu Manchu* starring Christopher Lee as the titular oriental villain. In later years, Sir Christopher Lee would become perhaps my ultimate acting hero and I finally realised my ambition of meeting the great man in 2003. What a treasured moment that was. I was excited and nervous in equal measures. He was an absolute gentleman with an aura about him that only true stars have.

My ninth birthday was probably my most memorable as a child, even more so than when I entered double figures the following year. On the day I turned nine, I received the greatest present I could wish for, an adorable Labrador puppy called Major. This excitable, playful, affectionate, downright daft-as-a-brush dog quickly became my best friend and remained so for the next sixteen years. I couldn't have asked for a better companion to grow up alongside.

Looking at the BBC schedules for that day in 1979, there isn't a lot to fuel my personal nostalgia tank. One programme does stand out however, bringing a lot of memories flooding back, particularly of the theme tune. That programme is *The Water Margin*. A Japanese production dubbed into English, *The Water Margin* was an action series set in ancient China, the story based on a classic tale from Chinese literature of 108 knights being reborn to fight the tyranny of the land's rulers.

The narration for the English version of *The Water Margin* was provided by the legendary Burt Kwouk. His wonderful delivery of various ancient and rather obscure Chinese proverbs was a constant highlight, alongside that magnificent theme tune of course. Just as hearing a pop tune can take you back to a precise moment in time, so too a familiar television theme has the capacity to transport you to a particular period of your life. Hearing the theme to this classic of Japanese television today, I am once again a primary school pupil, rushing to finish my homework before settling down to watch *The Water Margin,* a tray of fish fingers, mash and peas on my lap.

As a new decade arrived, I hit the double-figure mark. The big film on BBC1 on my birthday that year was some tosh starring Tom Skerritt called *Maneaters are Loose!* The plot, such as it was, involved a couple of man-eating tigers which escape from a zoo and terrorise a small Californian town. No doubt inspired by *Jaws,* it is a film that I have never seen or even heard of again since. Meanwhile, BBC2 was busy covering an international chess tournament, the blurb in the *Radio Times* for *The Master Game* exclaiming, 'Tonight a stiff examination awaits the pupil in front of his favourite professor!' Yes folks, chess really was a televised sport in those days.

In 1986, I turned sweet sixteen. On the day of that momentous occasion, a young Brian Turner was taking his first steps as a television chef on *Pebble Mill at One*, presenting a segment called *Budget Cookery.* The evening schedule on BBC1 featured an episode of the hugely popular sitcom *No Place Like Home* with William Gaunt and a young Martin Clunes, followed by another instalment of the mighty *Dallas,* of which there is plenty more later in the book.

When I officially became an adult in 1988, my birthday fell, quite nicely, on a Saturday. Children's Saturday morning television was still going strong at this point with Phillip Schofield, Sarah Greene and Gordon the Gopher at the helm of the popular *Going Live!* One of the guests on the show that day was a fourteen-year old Christian Bale, talking about his role in Steven Spielberg's *Empire of the Sun.*

Snooker was featured on both BBC1 and BBC2 as the World Team Cup reached its climax. England, their team comprised of the world's top three ranked players at the time, were the ultimate victors. The tournament was presented by a certain David Icke. I wonder whatever happened to him?

It really is fascinating to look at the television programmes that were being broadcast on key dates during the formative years of your life. More than any other entertainment medium, I believe that television adds an extra layer to your personality. The programmes that you grow up watching play a part in shaping the kind of person you will become in the future. This is particularly true of children's television, which, rather fittingly, we will look at next.

AS IF BY MAGIC – PROPER KIDS TELLY

Nothing fuels a nostalgia-soaked conversation amongst friends quite like a discussion concerning the television programmes which filled each day of our childhood. These warm recollections of our favourite children's shows of the past transport us back to a time when life seemed much simpler. As a nine-year old, one of the toughest decisions I regularly faced on a Saturday morning was deciding which of the Kellogg's Variety Pack cereals to eat, whilst switching television channels between *Multi-Coloured Swap Shop* and *Tiswas*. For the record, it was the Rice Krispies which were usually devoured first, whilst equal time was spent watching Noel Edmonds on BBC and Chris Tarrant on ATV (as it was known back then). Many children of the time were fiercely loyal to either *Swap Shop* or *Tiswas* but, just to be awkward, I was a fan of both. I enjoyed the anarchy and unpredictability of the latter but was equally content amongst the relative calm of Noel and fellow knitted jumper enthusiast John Craven on the good old BBC.

Of course, both of these bastions of children's Saturday morning television began in the seventies - *Tiswas* debuted in the Midland region in 1974, while *Multi-Coloured Swap Shop* was first broadcast in 1976 – and it is this very decade, along with the ensuing eighties, which I believe to be the Golden Age of Children's Television. With repeats of classic programmes from the sixties happily co-existing with newly broadcast wonders such as *Bagpuss*, *The*

Wombles and *Paddington*, the seventies really can lay claim to being the golden decade of children's television. I still retain a strong attachment to the shows from this era, as do many people from my generation. As reading was one of my passions as a kid, remaining so to this day, many of my favourite children's TV programmes from this era were based on original books.

For many of us who grew up in the seventies, there is one particular series of books which defined our childhood like no other – the *Mr Men* series. Written and illustrated by Roger Hargreaves, the *Mr Men* books were a continual source of delight for seventies kids and remain so today, with Roger's son Adam reviving the franchise in 1990 after a twelve year gap.

The very first of the *Mr Men* to appear on bookshelves was Mr Tickle in 1971. Roger Hargreaves was inspired to create the character after his young son Adam asked him what a tickle looked like. Thus, the rotund, long-armed Mr Tickle was born.

One of the great things about the *Mr Men* books was the fact that they only cost around 20p to buy, the perfect price for pocket-money conscious kids. The short length of each book was also ideal for the intended audience, as were the bright, colourful illustrations. Each story usually contained a moral which the main character learnt along the way, a useful lesson that led to the majority of us young readers growing up to be pretty well-adjusted too. Kind of...

With thirty-nine different characters each having their own book, completing the full set became irresistible to most of us. That is the beauty of having a large set of distinctive characters each with their own story. You just have to possess the full collection. Everybody had their favourite *Mr Men* characters.

I remember having a fondness for Mr Strong, Mr Fussy, Mr Uppity, Mr Bump and Mr Sneeze.

The BBC *Mr Men* animated television series, first broadcast on New Year's Eve 1974, brought the inhabitants of Misterland to life in a magical fashion. While Mr Tickle had the honour of being the first of the *Mr Men* to be immortalised in print, the first character to appear on screen was the ever jolly Mr Happy. Each episode of the television adaptation was an almost word-for-word replication of the book upon which it was based, which gave the proceedings a warm, familiar feel. Add to this the memorably deadpan, deliberately slow-paced narration of the ever-brilliant Arthur Lowe and it is easy to see why *Mr Men* retains a place in the hearts of those of us who were lucky enough to be around when the series was first broadcast.

Alongside *Mr Men,* there was another series of books which captured my imagination as a child – *Paddington Bear*. It was back in 1958 that the world was first introduced to the little bear with impeccable manners and a penchant for marmalade sandwiches. Michael Bond worked as a cameraman for the BBC at the time but was also a keen writer. One Christmas, while looking for a gift for his wife in Selfridges, he came across a teddy bear sitting all alone on a shelf with no other toys to keep him company. Taking pity upon the lonesome bear, Bond took him home and thus, the idea for a series of books which have captivated both children and adults alike for over half a century was born.

The first Paddington book, *A Bear Called Paddington*, was published in 1958. This most enduring of children's literary characters has since featured in a further twenty-seven books. In 2014, a whole new audience was introduced to the lovable

A Royal Mail stamp from 2006 featuring the loveable Paddington Bear. (Photo: Netfali/Shutterstock)

bear as he made his debut on the big screen in *Paddington*. Unlike many other modern film updates of classic television series or books, *Paddington* is an absolute joy, retaining all of the charm and likability of its seventies forerunner. Author Michael Bond even makes a heart-warming cameo. So successful was the *Paddington* movie, an equally enjoyable sequel was released in 2017, although this time there would be no appearance from the loveable bear's creator, as Bond had passed away a few months before at the grand age of 91.

As a child, I was utterly captivated by the adventures and unintentional mishaps of the well-meaning bear. I loved that Paddington was so utterly polite too. He always raised his hat, never failed to say please and thank you and only used his trademark 'hard stare' when totally necessary. A perfect role model for youngsters in many ways. It's a shame that there aren't more role models like Paddington around today.

As with the *Mr Men*, the Paddington Bear character got his own BBC television show, simply called *Paddington*. The utterly adorable bear first raised his hat on BBC1 in the early evening of Monday 5 January 1976, 17:40pm to be precise. From Monday to Friday, 17:40pm was a highly significant time for all telly-watching kids, as it represented the last chance each day for us to enjoy our very own programmes before the monotony of the National News took over at 17:45pm. Although I found the news terribly dull when I was young, the likes of Richard Baker, Kenneth Kendall, Peter Woods and Richard Whitmore still became hugely familiar figures to me at the time. None of them could compare to Paddington Bear though, even Richard Baker, who also happened to be the voice of *Mary, Mungo and Midge*.

Right from the outset, the memorable theme tune perfectly encapsulated the gentle, leisurely nature of *Paddington*, while the gloriously smooth voice of renowned thespian Sir Michael Hordern, sitting in the narrator's chair, added both depth of character and a touch of undoubted class to the proceedings. The fact that only Paddington Bear himself was animated using the stop-motion process, while all of the other characters were flat 2-D drawings, made this marmalade-loving, hard-stare-giving Peruvian bear all the more real to young eyes.

The stop-motion technique added depth to characters in terms of both physical presence and a child's emotional attachment. The more real a character seemed, the greater the love younger viewers would shower upon it. A prime example of this was the lead character in, quite possibly, the greatest children's television programme ever made - *Bagpuss*.

There have been a number of polls conducted over the years on the subject of the nation's favourite kids TV show. In the vast majority of these polls *Bagpuss* is invariably ranked in the top five and in many cases occupies the very top spot. The series is richly deserving of that lofty status too, especially when you consider it attained such iconic status in the space of a mere thirteen episodes.

Unlike its contemporaries *Mr Men* and *Paddington*, the narration for *Bagpuss* was not provided by a well-known actor of the day. Instead, voice-over duties were handled by Oliver Postgate, a writer and animator who, along with Peter Firmin, ran the animation company Smallfilms which produced *Bagpuss*, in addition to other enduring children's television classics such as *Ivor the Engine* and *The Clangers*.

Even now, over forty years since I first settled down in front of the television to watch *Bagpuss*, the tender, soothing tones of Oliver Postgate retain the ability to wrap warmly around me like a winter blanket. I am immediately transported back to a time when I would be completely engrossed in the gentle adventures of the good-natured saggy cloth cat and his friends; well educated bookend Professor Yaffle the owl, kindly ragdoll Madeleine, Gabriel the guitar-playing toad and, of course, the energetic mice with their Marvellous Mechanical Mouse Organ.

The series was set in a shop owned by a young girl called Emily. The shop was unique in that, rather than actually selling things, it was stocked with items that people had lost. As I grew older and my inner cynic unfortunately expanded accordingly, I began to wonder how the shop managed to remain open if nothing was ever actually sold? Just how did the business make any money? Luckily, the innocence of childhood rendered such trivial matters meaningless.

After Emily brought a new item in to the shop each episode, so the previously inanimate cloth cat would magically come to life, followed by each of his friends. Tales would be told and songs sang, all revolving around the latest addition to the shop's wares. Classic episodes that I recall with fondness include the one where the mice use a working miniature model of a mill to make a seemingly endless supply of chocolate biscuits (they are, in fact, rotating the same biscuit) and also one which features a fiddle-playing leprechaun who lives in an upturned metal bucket and smokes trout for his supper.

As with the majority of children's programmes recalled in this chapter, and indeed most of the output from this era, *Bagpuss* was gentle and warm, each story unfolding at a leisurely pace, allowing young viewers plenty of time to take in the story and thus become totally enraptured by the magic unfolding before them.

The slower pace and gentle story-telling style of *Bagpuss* was a hallmark of Smallfilms output, a tradition that began with their debut production, *Ivor the Engine*, in 1959. The first series of *Ivor the Engine* was broadcast in black and white on the ITV network.

Many of these early episodes were remade in colour in the mid-seventies, this time on the BBC, thereby introducing the endearing Welsh steam engine to a whole new audience, of which I was a happy member.

Once again, the warm narration of Oliver Postgate ensured that *Ivor the Engine* would take its rightful place in the pantheon of children's television greats, in addition to occupying a permanent spot in the memory of every child of the seventies.

The adventures of little green engine Ivor, his driver Jones the Steam and pet dragon Idris will always retain a special place in my heart. The Welsh setting was a happy coincidence for me as my father was born in Wales. Although the town in which *Ivor the Engine* was set was entirely fictional, it was said to be located in the 'top left-hand corner of Wales'. My father was from South Wales, the opposite end of the country. Despite this however, the small village in which he was born, a former mining community, was similar in so many ways to Ivor's home town of Llaniog. The fictional inhabitants of Llaniog, including Dai Station, Evans the Song and Mrs Griffiths, were a very tight-knit bunch and very community-spirited. The same can be said for the very real village of Abergwnfi, where my father was born. Everybody knew each other and it was almost as if the town and its occupants existed happily in their own world, a small community independent from the rest of the nation.

Whilst on a personal level I could equate the Wales depicted in *Ivor the Engine* to the real Wales that I knew as a child, Oliver Postgate himself was partly inspired, at least in terms of setting, by the works of legendary Welsh poet Dylan Thomas. It was the likes of *Under Milk Wood,* along with the very real mountain railways which exist throughout Wales, that determined this part of the UK as the ideal setting for this most memorable of children's classics.

Another glorious entry in the list of utterly captivating children's television series of the seventies was *The Wombles*. First appearing in a series of books by Elizabeth Beresford, Wombles were little furry creatures who, in addition to being highly active, also happened to be extremely environmentally friendly. Their main aim in life was to 'make good use of bad rubbish', in particular that which was left behind on Wimbledon Common. The theme of recycling was certainly ahead of its time and the message of being kind to the environment was an important one to get across to younger viewers.

Although the books had already been a success in their own right, the popularity of these adorable, busy little creatures went into overdrive when the first episode of the stop-motion animated television series was broadcast on the BBC on Monday 5 February 1973. The time of broadcast? Yes, you've guessed it – 17:40pm. A range of merchandise soon followed and there was even a Wombles pop band. In 1974 alone, The Wombles reached number 4 in the UK singles chart with *The Wombling Song*, number 3 with *Remember You're a Womble* and then enjoyed a huge festive hit when *Wombling Merry Christmas* reached number 5 in the yuletide chart, before peaking at number 2 in January 1975.

I was a huge fan of *The Wombles* at the time. Although I can't recall exactly how old I would have been, possibly around six or seven, I have a vivid memory of receiving a birthday cake topped with little plastic Womble figures. I kept the figure of Great Uncle Bulgaria for years afterwards, right up until adulthood. In fact, I would probably still have it now if it hadn't been lost when my future wife and I moved in to our first house together.

Each episode of *The Wombles* was a mere five minutes in length but plenty of magic was created in that brief running time. Many of the episodes revolved around items that the Wombles came across during their daily duties. The stories were simple but effective and included Orinoco being swept away by an umbrella on a windy day, Wellington using a cardboard box to hide from a human being and Great Uncle Bulgaria reliving his youth by playing football.

A lot of the credit for the long-lasting popularity of *The Wombles* television series must go to the wonderful Bernard Cribbins, whose softly-spoken, sweet narration has remained indelibly printed in the memories of all seventies kids. Although he has accomplished so much during his long, varied and immensely successful career, whenever I hear the voice of Bernard Cribbins today, I am a child once more, fighting an almost irresistible urge to grab a shoulder pouch and venture out into the street to search for litter.

Along with Messrs. Cribbins, Lowe, Hordern and Postgate, the voice of actor Ray Brooks was a comforting, familiar part of the television soundtrack during the early seventies. Brooks provided the narration for one of the most fondly recalled TV shows of the time.

Indeed, no discussion of classic children's television shows from this era is complete without mentioning a certain pinstripe-suit clad, bowler hatted resident of Festive Road. The eponymous *Mr Benn* was a fairly unremarkable man at first glance, you might say even a tad bland. However, as soon as he stepped into the changing room of his local fancy dress shop, where the shopkeeper would always appear 'as if by magic', the unassuming Mr Benn transformed into a bit of a hero.

From cowboy to clown and pirate to caveman, the costumes that Mr Benn tried on dictated the adventure which he would have each episode. The episodes of which I have the strongest memory include one in which our hero joins in a game of hide and seek in the wild west and also the very first episode, which sees Mr Benn dress as a medieval knight in order to help a friendly dragon regain the trust of his king.

As with *Bagpuss*, *Mr Benn* has attained iconic status within the world of children's television on the strength of just thirteen episodes. Our continued attachment to *Mr Benn* is perhaps best exemplified by the bowler-hatted hero remaining the character with which Ray Brooks is still most identified, almost fifty years after the first episode was broadcast. In another similarity with the saggy pink cloth cat, *Mr Benn* appealed to a wide age-range of children, from pre-schoolers to those entering those awkward teenage years. This was also true for the next programme on my nostalgic list - *Rainbow*

Although the main demographic to which *Rainbow* was targeted was that of pre-school children, it was one of those programmes that appealed to all ages, even adults. With more than 1000 episodes broadcast over a twenty-year period, *Rainbow* is right up there as one of the most beloved children's television series of all-time.

The influence of *Rainbow* on popular British culture cannot be underestimated, with so many of the show's characters, human or otherwise, going on to become cult figures which still retain their popularity today. Ask anyone over the age of thirty-five if they know who Zippy is and you are likely to get a full impersonation of the loveable rascal in response. The same could be said for gentle pink hippo George too. Matching George in the colour stakes was Geoffrey Hayes with his headache-inducing trousers, usually coloured either bright yellow or a fierce shade of red. Then, of course, there is that magnificent theme tune, a beautifully nostalgic reminder of weekday lunchtimes during the seventies, 12:10pm to be exact, when you would happily sing along to that eternally happy melody.

Up above the streets and houses,
Rainbow climbing high,
Everyone can see it smiling
Over the sky
Paint the whole world with a rainbow...

The aim of *Rainbow* was to educate young viewers, mainly in terms of language skills and numbers, while also teaching the importance of various life values such as sharing, forgiveness and being polite. Often a dispute would arise between Zippy, George and Bungle which Geoffrey would aim to resolve through stories and song. One matter which was never resolved however concerned our big bear friend Bungle (or Bungle-Bonce as Zippy memorably called him). Bungle happily walked around naked during the day, as all bears do, but when it came to bedtime he insisted on donning pyjamas. Why? I am sure I am not the only person who has gamely wrestled with that baffling mystery all the way through to adulthood.

As *Rainbow* was really aimed at pre-school kids, the weekday pre-lunchtime broadcast slot to which it was allocated made perfect sense. The majority of the show's target audience would have spent an enjoyable morning at playschool before settling down for some fun with Zippy and the gang. This start time was also handy for older kids who happened to be off school suffering from some illness, whether real or greatly embellished. You could stay wrapped up in bed recovering from whatever ailment you were supposed to have, before making your way downstairs, still clad in pyjamas and cloaked in the duvet, just in time for *Rainbow* to begin. If the end of the week was approaching and you still had not gone back to school, you could always try to persuade your mom to let you stay off until after the weekend, in order to fully recover. After all, what would be the point in going back to school for just one day? You would only be off for another two days straight after that anyway.

I remember waiting for each weekend to roll around with much anticipation when I was younger. Saturday morning television was the highlight of the week for us kids during the seventies and eighties, as indeed it was for many adults too. While today's Saturday morning schedules are awash with cooking programmes, back in the *Proper Telly* era the first day of the weekend, as we shall now see, was the domain of the kid.

Although originally broadcast in its native United States in 1968 under the title *The Banana Splits Adventure Hour*, one of the most beloved of children's shows did not air in the UK until 1970, its title then being shortened to simply *The Banana Splits*.

The first live action show to be produced by Hanna Barbera, the masters of animation, *The Banana Splits* was a simply magical mix of slapstick comedy, songs, cartoons and men dressed in large animal costumes. Not to mention one of the greatest theme tunes in the

Promotional art for The Banana Splits Band (Image: Hanna-Barbera)

history of television. What more could your average seventies kid want?

When the BBC first broadcast *The Banana Splits* it was allocated the Friday teatime slot around 5pm. In 1971 it was moved to Saturday lunchtime just before *Grandstand* and would also be broadcast in the week during school holidays. As 1980 arrived, *The Banana Splits* was repeated early on a Saturday morning and it is these showings of which I have the fondest memory. Saturday mornings on the BBC really were special back then. *The Banana Splits* would be followed by either *Champion the Wonder Horse, Zorro* or the French adventure serial *The Flashing Blade*. Wonderful times.

I remember coming downstairs early each Saturday morning, still clad in my pyjamas, in order to watch the latest adventures of Bingo, Fleagle, Drooper and Snorky, who made up the Banana Splits Band. Just in case you can't remember who was who, Bingo was the gorilla who played the drums, Fleagle was the guitar-wielding dog, Drooper was a bass-playing lion, while keyboards were taken care of by Snorky the elephant. In the famous theme song, Snorky's name was shortened to simply Snork.

I have so many great memories of *The Bananas Splits*, perhaps more so than any other children's show from that era; the hilarious antics of the main characters and the over the top sound effects which accompanied each slapstick moment, that legendary theme tune which you just can't get out of your head and also the regular cartoons *Arabian Knights* and *The Three Musketeers*. The show also featured a live action adventure serial called *Danger Island* which starred Jan-Michael Vincent. Interestingly, the director of *Danger Island* was Richard Donner, who would go on to direct such huge films as *Superman*, *The Goonies* and *Lethal Weapon*.

Footage of the Banana Splits Band driving mini cars called Banana Buggies and enjoying various theme park rides was used for the opening credits and also for mini musical segments within each show. These pieces of live footage were filmed at Six Flags Over Texas in Arlington, Texas, a theme park which remains open to this day.

Nearly forty years after first watching *The Banana Splits*, it remains one of my ambitions to drive a Banana Buggy. These most fun-looking of vehicles were, in reality, customised Amphicats, six-wheel-drive amphibious all-terrain vehicles. Sadly, the Amphicat ceased production in 1975, so any existing models still in good running order are probably in short supply. Looks like I will never realise my dream after all.

The one and only Noel Edmonds, a fixture of Saturday morning television during the Proper Telly era. (Photo: Paul Box)

While *The Banana Splits* and *Champion the Wonder Horse* were integral parts of the Saturday morning schedule during the summer months, they were really only keeping the slot warm for the autumn return of the true bastion of children's Saturday morning television, *Multi-Coloured Swap Shop*.

First broadcast at the beginning of October 1976, *Swap Shop* was, in many ways, a trailblazer for Saturday morning children's television. Although perennial rival *Tiswas* had actually debuted two years previously in 1974, this was only in the Midlands region, so was yet to become a national phenomenon. As a result, it was *Swap Shop* which really set the benchmark for all weekend children's shows to follow.

Every Saturday morning, starting from around 9:30am, cuddly Noel Edmonds would be at the helm for more than three hours of live fun. Each week, there would be star guests answering viewers questions over the telephone, news segments from John Craven, cartoons and, of course, the chance for youngsters to swap any unwanted items in their possession with likeminded viewers who had other delights they wished to get rid of.

Swaps were either done in the studio, where Noel would read out telephone swap requests, or famously, on outside broadcasts from around the country, hosted by the late Keith Chegwin. These Swaporama events would often be attended by thousands of eager young fans, who would tune in to *Swap Shop* first thing in order to find out where Keith was going to be that week. Remember, this was in the days before the internet existed, so there was less chance of the location for the latest Swaporama event leaking out beforehand. This made the final reveal a lot more exciting.

Each week, the celebrity guests in the studio would bring along a prize that viewers could win by answering a question put forth by the celebrity. Answers had to be written on a postcard, which would then be drawn live on air the following week from a giant clear plastic globe. The postcards would usually be of all shapes and sizes, with many children hoping that their distinctive postcard would catch the eye of the person making the draw. That ploy never seemed to work though, as the guests making the draw would often be distracted by Noel's chatter. This kind of competition, requiring you to send in your answers by post, is now sadly defunct. Mention the phrase 'answers on a postcard' to kids nowadays and you will receive the blankest of blank stares in return. Sadly they will never get to experience the simple pleasure of popping a freshly-written postcard through the slot of the post-box at the end of the street, in the vain hope that a signed copy of the latest vinyl LP by Adam Ant would be sent in return.

I never did win a record by Mr Ant, or any other *Swap Shop* competition prize for that matter. Not that I really entered that many in all honesty. One thing I am positive I never actually did was telephone Noel on the show, either to ask a famous guest a question or put in a swap request. However, despite never dialling it, the telephone number for *Multi-Coloured Swap Shop* will linger in my memory for the rest of my days. Seventies children, chant along with me - 01 811 8055.

From the mid-seventies to the early eighties, viewers of Saturday morning television were divided into two camps. You were either a *Swap Shop* kid or a *Tiswas* kid. As I've already mentioned, being the awkward type, I was actually a fan of both. If I could only choose one now, I may well just come down on the side of Noel but it would be a close run thing.

Although *Multi-Coloured Swap Shop* had some moments of anarchy and unpredictability being a live show, it was nothing compared to the antics of Chris Tarrant and the rest of the crew over on the commercial network. *Tiswas* was akin to the naughty schoolchild who would always take their seat at the back of the classroom, while *Swap Shop* more closely resembled a front seat kid.

Living in the Midlands region, we were able to tune into *Tiswas* right from the very first episode. Viewers in the rest of the country had to wait varying amounts of time until their local network picked it up. Some regions didn't begin broadcasting the programme until 1979, five years after it first aired. This is why

Swap Shop is regarded by many as the forerunner for live Saturday morning television, despite *Tiswas* actually being the first to air.

Every episode of *Tiswas* was organised chaos and kids lapped it up. It wasn't just younger viewers who tuned in either. Dads up and down the country would happily sit and watch with their kids in order to await the appearance of a certain Sally James. The lovely Sally, usually clad in denim or leather trousers, was the main co-host of the show, alongside a young Chris Tarrant, who of course would go on to become one of the most famous presenters on British television. In addition to Chris and Sally, the *Tiswas* presenting team also consisted of such names as Lenny Henry, John Gorman and Bob Carolgees, along with his friend Spit the Dog.

The guests on *Tiswas*, particularly the musical ones, weren't always what you would expect on a children's show. For instance, the heavy rock band Motorhead, led by the inimitable Lemmy, were semi-regular guests and their appearances, along with those of fellow rockers Status Quo, were usually accompanied by Chris Tarrant excitedly proclaiming straight to camera, "This is what they want!"

One of the most fondly remembered *Tiswas* features was The Cage, inside which kids and sometimes their parents would be locked and then soaked with buckets of water. Presenters, studio audience members and star guests would also be prone to attack by the shadowy, black-clad figure The Phantom Flan Flinger, whose stock of custardy flans were in seemingly permanent supply.

By the end of the seventh series in 1981, Chris Tarrant had left *Tiswas* in order to front a late night adult version of the show called *O.T.T.* Lenny Henry, John Gorman and Bob Carolgees all went with him, leaving just Sally James remaining from the main *Tiswas* presenting team. She was joined on series eight by Midlands radio personality Gordon Astley but the writing was on the wall and *Tiswas* duly ended in 1982. Saturday mornings would certainly never be the same again but what about Sundays?

During the eighties, *Bullseye* host Jim Bowen often stated that Sundays wouldn't be the same without a bit of Bully. In the preceding decade, it could be said that Sundays were not the same without a bit of muppetry. The memorable *Muppet Show* theme tune, a brilliant pastiche of big musical numbers, was the soundtrack to my childhood Sunday afternoons.

Although the creation of Mississippi-born master puppeteer Jim Henson, *The Muppet Show* was actually a British/American co-production. After network executives in the States proved to be unsure about the show after viewing the pilot, UK television executive Lew Grade invited Henson to make the

Sunday afternoons were never the same without The Muppet Show. (Photo: The Muppets Studio,LLC)

series at Elstree Studios for the ATV franchise. *The Muppet Show* was then subsequently sold back to American networks.

Despite US TV executives missing a trick with *The Muppet Show* (especially as *Sesame Street*, which featured Henson's muppets, was so popular), I didn't mind as it meant we got to see the show first. From 1976 to 1981, *The Muppet Show* was appointment viewing in our house. I have a vivid memory of owning a homemade Kermit the Frog glove puppet, while my cousin had one of Fozzie Bear. I'm not sure whether it was my mom or my cousin's mom who made them but I do remember that they were both pretty damn awesome.

The popularity of Kermit, Fozzie, Miss Piggy, Gonzo and the rest of the gang has not really diminished to any great degree since *The Muppet Show* first hit our screens back in September 1976. The gang returned to television during the nineties with *The Muppets Tonight* and then again in 2015 for one series of *The Muppets*. The franchise has also proved popular in cinemas with eight big screen outings so far, from *The Muppet Movie* in 1979 to *The Muppets Most Wanted* in 2015, the latter guest-starring Ricky Gervais.

Speaking of guest stars, one of the things which always impressed me about The *Muppet Show* was the amazing calibre of celebrities which appeared throughout the five series. Each week would see a different special guest helping the muppets with their theatre production. Watching the show as a child, I was introduced to a whole new world of superstars from film and music, some who would go on to be favourites of mine as I grew up.

Just to emphasise the incredible talent which appeared on *The Muppet Show*, here is a list of just a few of the amazing guests from the programme's five-year run.

Vincent Price, Dudley Moore, Dom DeLuise, Roger Moore, Diana Ross, Elton John, Steve Martin, Peter Ustinov, George Burns, Bruce Forsyth, John Cleese, Bob Hope, Peter Sellers, Julie Andrews, Alice Cooper, Liberace, Cheryl Ladd, Cloris Leachman, Raquel Welch, Danny Kaye, Spike Milligan, Sylvester Stallone, Kenny Rogers, Liza Minnelli, Lynda Carter, Christopher Reeve, James Coburn, Shirley Bassey, Gladys Knight, Johnny Cash and Gene Kelly.

That is just a small sample of the great calibre of guest star that *The Muppet Show* managed to attract. For many children of the time, myself included, this would be the first time that we had come across many of these people. What a fantastic way to be introduced to such talent!

I am eternally grateful to my parents for ensuring that I was born in the year that I was. This lovely bit of timing ensured I could enjoy first-hand some of the greatest kid's telly shows ever made. I was there to witness first-hand the Golden Age of Children's Television, the like of which we will never see again.
Watching some of these classic programmes once more – all in the name of research of course - and reliving some wonderful childhood memories in the process has put a spring in my step and a smile in my heart. Writing about each and every one of these TV treasures could easily take up an entire book in itself, which is why I have concentrated on just a few. However, it would be amiss of me to finish this

chapter without mentioning some of the other wonderful shows that helped make me the person I am today.

For example, how could I not mention the legend that is Basil Brush? In 2018, this most charming and urbane of foxes celebrated his fiftieth year in show business. During the seventies, *The Basil Brush Show* was essential Saturday teatime viewing. Basil had various human companions over the years including Mr Rodney (Likely Lad star Rodney Bewes), Mr Derek (Derek Fowlds) and Mr Roy (Roy North).

Puppets were integral to many great children's shows during the seventies. One of the most popular of these shows was *Pipkins*. The star of the show was the endearingly scruffy Hartley Hare who, along with his friends Topov the monkey, Pig, Tortoise and Octavia the ostrich, ran the Helping People organisation. Broadcast each weekday lunchtime, Pipkins remains one of the most treasured TV memories for seventies kids. Hartley was a brilliant character, somewhat reminiscent of legendary comedic film cad Terry-Thomas.

Puppets of a far simpler nature were the stars of *Fingerbobs*. Coming to life via the hands of human companion Yoffy, finger puppet Fingermouse and his friends Gulliver the seagull, Flash the tortoise and Scampi the...er...scampi would usually spend each episode collecting various objects from which another item would be created. First broadcast under the *Watch with Mother* umbrella on BBC2 in 1972, *Fingerbobs* was shown frequently throughout the rest of the decade, despite only thirteen episodes being made. With his thick dark beard, balding dome and piercing eyes, Canadian actor Rick Jones, who played Yoffy, may seem now to be an unlikely children's telly favourite. However, his soft Canadian accent and velvet voice were the ideal accompaniment to the adventures of Fingermouse and friends and he was always a popular and reassuring presence on *Play School*. Today, great presenters like Rick Jones would sadly never get the chance to front children's television shows. It seems that, in order to make it as a kid's presenter in the modern world, you need to have the facial complexion of a new-born baby and possess a speaking voice which sounds as if you are permanently hooked up to a tank of helium.

Just think, if that had been the criteria back in the *Proper Telly* era, we would never have had the pleasure of watching the likes of dear Johnny Morris on *Animal Magic* or the wonderful Tony Hart on *Take Hart*. That is truly unthinkable.

Not all of my favourite childhood programmes were broadcast on BBC. Over on ITV, classics such as *Chorlton and the Wheelies*, *Jamie and the Magic Torch* and *Danger Mouse* left an indelible print on the hearts of many a kid. These three bastions of kids telly were all produced by the wonderful animation studio Cosgrove Hall. Founded by Brian Cosgrove and Mark Hall, Cosgrove Hall Productions are responsible for some of the greatest children's series of all-time. In addition to the three programmes already mentioned, the studio can also boast *Count Duckula*, *The Wind in the Willows* and *Cockleshell Bay* amongst its other productions. What a back catalogue that is and what a wonderful time to be a kid.

DRAT AND DOUBLE DRAT –
PROPER CARTOONS

With notable exceptions such as *The Banana Splits* and *Sesame Street*, the vast majority of live-action children's television shows broadcast in the UK during the seventies were home-grown. When it came to cartoons however, the situation was reversed. Most of the animated series which we enjoyed during this time were produced across the pond in the USA.

Animated series produced in the UK at the time were mainly of the stop-motion variety with flat 2D characters moving across stationary backgrounds. Popular examples of this fairly primitive but nevertheless endearing style were *Ivor the Engine, Mr Benn, Bod* and *Mary, Mungo and Midge*. All of these productions were incredibly successful of course and are now, quite rightly, considered as classics of the genre. However, their popularity amongst the young television viewing public of the seventies was about to be challenged by an invasion from across the Atlantic.

While the British pop invasion of the USA during the sixties was led by The Beatles, the reciprocal American raid of British children's television was helmed by the legendary Hanna-Barbera.

Animators William Hanna and Joseph Barbera first met when working for MGM during the forties, their desks fortuitously located opposite one another. The first collaborative production from the young pair resulted in the creation of arguably the most famous animated double act of all-time, *Tom and Jerry*.

Although the name of producer Fred Quimby was prevalent on the credits for *Tom and Jerry* cartoons, it was Hanna and Barbera who were the real creative force behind the feuding cat and mouse.

When MGM decided to close its animated division in 1957, Hanna and Barbera decided to form their own animation production company, specialising in making cartoons for the medium of television. An early success for the new, official Hanna-Barbera partnership was *The Huckleberry Hound Show*. This was quickly followed by one of the company's most enduring creations, *The Flintstones*. First airing in the US in the autumn of 1960, *The Flintstones*, itself based on the live-action comedy series *The Honeymooners,* pioneered the idea of animated sitcoms, paving the way for the likes of *The Simpsons* and *Family Guy*.

The huge success of *The Flintstones* also led to Hanna-Barbera producing more animated series featuring episodes of a longer running length, mirroring those of standard live-action comedy shows. Classic examples of this strategy included *Top Cat, The Jetsons, Wait Till Your Father Gets Home, Inch High Private Eye* and *Godzilla*.

While I loved watching all of these (especially *Top Cat*), the following Hanna-Barbera productions retain a special place in my nostalgic memory bank.

A big, lovable Great Dane with a cast-iron stomach was the star of arguably my all-time favourite cartoon series, *Scooby-Doo, Where Are You?* The loveable mutt definitely occupies top spot in my personal list of greatest cartoon characters. Although of a nervous disposition, particularly where ghosts were concerned, the Scoobster possessed a fierce sense of loyalty to his friends; the seemingly permanently dazed Shaggy, handsome group leader Fred, damsel in distress Daphne and the intelligent Velma, who was usually the one to eventually solve each mystery.

Everyone's favourite ghost-chasing canine made his first on-screen appearance in the US on September 13 1969 as the part of the CBS network's revised Saturday morning schedules. *Scooby Doo, Where Are You?* had undergone a number of title changes before making it to air, including the rather bland *Mysteries Five* and the clumsy *Who's S-S Scared?* Even Scooby Doo himself had not been immune to the name-change treatment, thanks to a little-known singer who went by the name of Frank Sinatra. Originally, our canine hero was known as Too Much. Yes I know, what kind of an awful name is that? Legend tells that, whilst travelling by plane to a meeting, CBS executive Fred Silverman was listening to a recording of *Strangers in the Night* by Sinatra and was inspired by the 'doo-be-doo-be-doo' phrasing which closed out the song. Another story has animator Iwao Takamoto as the man taking inspiration from Sinatra's 'doo-be-doo' ad lib. Whatever the correct version of the story, Too Much was out and Scooby Doo was in.

Scooby Doo, Where Are You? ran for twenty-five glorious episodes. Each show adhered to very much the same format, a template that further Scooby Doo series would follow for years to come, becoming the cartoon's much-loved trademark. Travelling around in their van, the famous Mystery Machine, our gang of heroes would inevitably find themselves embroiled in a mystery involving a ghost or some kind of ghoulish monster terrorising an establishment, usually a run-down fairground or a dusty old museum. Best friends Scooby and Shaggy would often end up being chased by the creature in question before stumbling upon a vital clue. Each week's episode finished with the villainous monster being unmasked and revealed to be as human as you and I. The immortal line "I would have gotten away with it if it wasn't for you meddling kids!" retains a special place in the hearts of many of us.

The original *Scooby Doo, Where Are You?* remains the greatest of the various series featuring the cowardly but noble canine hero. Later efforts such as *The New Scooby Doo Movies* and *The 13 Ghosts of Scooby Doo* tinkered with the winning format and just didn't seem quite the same as a result. Then, of course, there was the introduction of Scooby's young nephew Scrappy Doo.

That poor young pup Scrappy must be one of the most hated cartoon characters in history. Everybody seemed to dislike him. Despite the negativity from fans, the addition of the plucky Scrappy Doo did revitalise the show's flagging ratings and, for a while, Scooby, Scrappy and Shaggy went it alone, without the aid of Fred, Daphne and Velma. Later series would see the whole gang reunited, albeit without the unpopular Scrappy.

Even though I am now well into my forties, I still possess a Scooby Doo t-shirt which I wear with pride. It brings a smile to everyone's face and that, after all, is what life should be all about. While Scooby was one of my cartoon heroes, I was not averse to cheering for the villains in other animated series.

For example, I am sure I was not the only kid who wished that the villainous duo of Dick Dastardly and his dog Muttley could occasionally be allowed to come out on top in *Wacky Races*. Despite being rascally cheats, they worked so hard to formulate and eventually implement their various schemes each week, you couldn't begrudge them the odd victory every now and then. Besides, how could anyone not love Muttley with his under-the-breath grumbles of dissatisfaction and that glorious wheezing laugh?

Dastardly and Muttley were just two of a plethora of distinct characters which populated the start line in each episode of the wonderful slapstick-filled *Wacky Races*. Debuting just twelve months before *Scooby Doo, Where Are You?*, *Wacky Races* was another winning formula from Hanna-Barbera Productions. Unlike the long-running Scooby Doo, *Wacky Races* lasted for a total of just seventeen episodes. However each of those episodes featured two car races, so we were always assured of double the fun every week!

Wacky Races arguably featured the largest cast of characters for any cartoon show, each desperately trying to win the coveted title of World's Wackiest Racer. With so many distinct characters, each with cars that mirrored their personalities and backgrounds, it was inevitable that, as viewers, we would develop favourites. As already mentioned, I always wanted Dastardly and Muttley to win but, alas, they never managed to enjoy the deliciously sweet taste of victory.

A dear friend of mine once told me that, as a child, he would write the results of each race down in a notebook, allocating points depending on finishing positions. Poor old Dastardly and Muttley never managed to score a single solitary point! To resolutely keep trying in the face of such adversity each week was a testament to the heart and willpower of the moustachioed rascal and his scruffy dog.

Incidentally, in terms of victories obtained, the most successful racers were The Ant Hill Mob, Penelope Pitstop, Luke and Blubber Bear and Peter Perfect, who all won four races each.

For telly nerds everywhere, of which I am a proud member, the full league table, with five points awarded for first place, three for second and one for third, is as follows:

1. The Slag Brothers   42
2. The Ant Hill Mob   37
3. Rufus Ruffcut & Sawtooth   37
4. Penelope Pitstop   31
5. The Red Max   30
6. The Gruesome Twosome   30
7. Peter Perfect   28
8. Luke and Blubber Bear   27
9. Professor Pat Pending   26
10. Sergeant Blast and Private Meekly 18
11. Dick Dastardly and Muttley   0

Along with the conniving duo of Dastardly and Muttley, The Slag Brothers, Rock and Gravel, were amongst the most popular of *Wacky Races* characters. The continually feuding, hair-covered Neanderthals served as inspiration for one of Hanna-Barbera's most enduring creations, *Captain Caveman*.

As perhaps befitting such a beloved animation as *Wacky Races*, particularly one with such an array of memorable characters, the acting talent involved with the production contained a number of legendary voice-over artists.

The distinctive, nasally tones of lead villain Dick Dastardly were provided by Paul Winchell, a well-known television personality in the States at the time, who had begun his career as a ventriloquist in the forties. In addition to Dastardly, Winchell provided the voice of Bubi Bear in another Hanna-Barbera favourite *Help!...It's the Hair Bear Bunch* and worked for Walt Disney on a number of Winnie the Pooh productions, memorably voicing the character of the loveable Tigger.

The frustrated grumbles and wheezing laugh of Muttley were provided by one of the all-time great voice actors, Don Messick. A Hanna-Barbera mainstay, Messick became something of a specialist when it came to voicing dogs, providing vocals for not only Muttley in *Wacky Races* but also futuristic canine Astro in *The Jetsons* and, perhaps most famously of all, the one and only Scooby Doo.

Yet another legendary name to appear on the credits of *Wacky Races* was that of Daws Butler. A long-time friend and colleague of Don Messick, Butler portrayed a number of the secondary characters in *Wacky Races*, including Peter Perfect, The Red Max and Rufus Ruffcut. Butler's list of voice credits is almost a who's who of classic cartoon characters - Yogi Bear, Huckleberry Hound, Barney Rubble, Quick Draw McGraw, Snagglepuss and Spike the Bulldog to name just a few.

On the subject of cartoon dogs, everybody's favourite animated canine superhero, *Hong Kong Phooey*, came along a little later than his fellow crime-fighting mutt Scooby Doo. Debuting in 1974, this evergreen classic amazingly ran for just sixteen episodes. However, much like *Wacky Races* before it, *Hong Kong Phooey* featured two separate stories each week.

As with so many of Hanna-Barbera's most popular cartoon series, *Hong Kong Phooey* was blessed with a truly memorable theme tune. In fact, I think this one may very well be my personal favourite Hanna-Barbera theme. Well, he is the 'number one super guy' after all.

Penry the pooch was a mild-mannered janitor who worked in the local police station. This was not your typical heavily-staffed police headquarters, as it seemed the only uniformed officers in situ were Rosemary, the shrill-voiced telephone operator and the often exasperated Sergeant Flint.

Rosemary was the first point of call for the reporting of crimes, the details of which Penry would often overhear. This would lead to the laid-back pooch secretly transforming himself into a crime-fighting superhero, via a complicated process involving an ironing board, a mattress springboard and a filing cabinet. Phooey was accompanied on his adventures by his faithful cat Spot, a seemingly lazy, almost inert feline who nevertheless possessed a sharp intellect which usually led to him saving the day, the completely oblivious Phooey being none the wiser to his companion's secret abilities..

I have so many happy childhood memories of watching *Hong Kong Phooey*. From the unforgettable theme tune and the *put-put-put* of our hero's car the wonderful 'phooeymobile', to the truly magnificent voice performances of the principle cast, in particular Scatman Crothers as the heroic pooch and Joe E. Ross as Sergeant Flint. Both Crothers and Ross had highly distinctive vocals perfectly suited to cartoon voice over duties.

Born in the state of Indiana in 1910, Benjamin Sherman Crothers acquired the nickname 'scatman' when he auditioned for a radio show in the early thirties. Although an accomplished jazz singer and musician, Crothers was perhaps best known for his many film appearances, including *One Flew Over the Cuckoo's Nest* and *The Shining* with Jack Nicholson and *Bronco Billy,* alongside Clint Eastwood. He also provided the voice of feline jazz-band leader Scat Cat in Disney's *The Aristocats,* performing the memorable song *Everybody Wants to be a Cat.*

Joe E Ross was a television veteran by the time *Hong Kong Phooey* went into production. The gravel-voiced comic rose to fame as Ritzik, the victim of many money-making scams perpetrated by a certain Sergeant Bilko in *The Phil Silvers Show.* He then went on to star in another hugely popular US television sitcom of the sixties, *Car 54, Where Are You?*

In both of these shows, Ross used his catchphrase 'Ooh! Ooh!' to great effect. The writers of *Hong Kong Phooey* incorporated the phrase into their scripts for the show, lending a feeling of warm familiarity to the character of Sergeant Flint. *Hong Kong Phooey* was not the only time that Joe E Ross got to utter 'Ooh! Ooh!' in animated form. He had already used those famous words to great effect a few years previously in another Hanna-Barbera classic, *Help!.. It's the Hair Bear Bunch.*

Although *Help!...It's the Hair Bear Bunch* made its debut in the States three years previously to *Hong Kong Phooey,* I have left it till last here because, on a personal level, this most wonderful of cartoon series is one that I discovered when I was a little older. When Hair Bear and his friends first appeared on British television – Friday 15 September 1972 at 16:55pm on BBC1 to be exact, I was only two years old, far too young to appreciate a cartoon such as this. More than likely, my initial encounter with these coolest of bears would have happened in 1978, when the series was reshown on BBC1 during the summer months.

Of the Hanna-Barbera output from the seventies, *Help!...It's the Hair Bear Bunch* has never really been a favourite of critics and is often overlooked when discussions concerning classic cartoon series get underway. However, on a personal level, it stands as one of my most fondly recalled cartoon shows.

Hair, Square and Bubi were three bears who resided at Wonderland Zoo. The cave in which they lived was secretly kitted out with lavish furnishings and mod cons. Whenever they were visited by head zookeeper Mr Peevly and his rather dim-witted assistant Botch, the bears flicked a switch to transform their cave back to its natural, unfurnished state.

Usually under the guidance of their shrewd leader Hair, the bears often escaped from the zoo, outwitting Peevly and Botch in the process, although they always returned to the comfort of their cave. The bears also possessed an invisible motorcycle which helped them escape from danger on a regular basis. As far as I can recall, the origins of this amazing piece of machinery were never explained.

At thirty minutes running time per episode, *Help!...It's the Hair Bear Bunch* had the feel of a traditional live-action sitcom (albeit one with talking bears and invisible motorcycles). In this respect, it followed on from preceding Hanna-Barbera productions such as *The Flintstones* and *The Jetsons*. In fact, it could be argued that the setup for the *Hair Bear Bunch* was partly inspired by *The Phil Silvers Show*. The legendary Daws Butler, who voiced Hair Bear, was said to have modelled the vocal mannerisms of the bear's leader on Bilko himself.

As with all Hanna-Barbera animated productions, the voice talent assembled for *Help!...It's the Hair Bear Bunch* was top-notch. In addition to the aforementioned Daws Butler, who was superb as the wily Hair Bear, Dick Dastardly himself, Paul Winchell, provided the sometimes unintelligible gobbledegook ramblings of the strange but nonetheless friendly Bubi Bear.

One of the greatest carton catchphrases of all-time came courtesy of the giant, slow-witted assistant zookeeper Lionel Botch, voiced by Joe E Ross. The actor's popular catchphrase of "Ooh! Ooh!" was lengthened slightly here by the addition of the name of Botch's boss. Adopting your best gruff voice, exclaim "Ooh! Ooh! Mr Peevly!" to anyone over the age of forty and I guarantee that they will not only know exactly what you mean but also where the phrase originated.

Once again, I could probably write an entire book on the great cartoon series which aired during the *Proper Telly* era. The ones I have written about in detail in this chapter remain my personal favourites and are the shows which have brought me the most pleasure over the years. However, here are the names of just a few more Hanna-Barbera classics from the same era which may well be on your own personal list of favourites:

Inch High Private Eye; *Wait Till Your Father Gets Home*; *Dastardly and Muttley in their Flying Machines*; *Josie and the Pussycats*; *Godzilla*; *Captain Caveman and the Teen Angels*; *Goober and the Ghostchasers*.

ANOTHER NICE MESS – PROPER AFTERNOON TELLY

If there is one part of modern day television which could be said to be *almost* on par with that of the *Proper Telly* era, it is afternoon television. The twenty-first century has seen the afternoon schedules become the domain of the quiz show. Prime time for quiz shows has shifted from the early evening slot favoured in the seventies to the preferred mid to late afternoon of today. Programmes such as *Tenable, Perfection, The Link, House of Games* and *Eggheads* are all hugely watchable, while the two big hitters of the afternoon quiz world, *Pointless* and *The Chase*, continue to fly high in the ratings.

As the author of a number of trivia books, I enjoy watching all of the shows listed above, particularly *Pointless*, which benefits hugely from the charming interplay between real-life long-time friends Alexander Armstrong and Richard Osman, who each possess an easy-going charm which puts contestants at ease. With quizzes and trivia being long-standing passions of mine, I probably would have been an avid watcher of this type of afternoon telly had it been popular back in the early to mid-eighties when I was a schoolboy. Indeed, one of my favourite afternoon shows during that time was *Blockbusters,* one of the very few quiz programmes which aired in the pre-tea time slot in those days. Instead, quiz and game shows were more regularly shown during the evening schedules. The afternoon till early evening slots were instead reserved for children's television, Japanese imports and Australian soaps. While this doesn't seem like the most enticing mix on paper - in fact you could be forgiven for thinking much of it to be pure trash - at the time it was a magical concoction. Honestly, it was.

I would usually get home from school around 3:30 in the afternoon. After a quick swig of ice-cold milk from the fridge – by the way, the milk had to be cold or I wouldn't touch it (that was the beauty of proper milk bottles) - I would begin my telly viewing afternoon, taking a break in-between to complete the dreaded but necessary chore of completing my school homework.

For some reason, I have a distinct memory of struggling to complete a particular homework assignment given during my final year at primary school. We had been asked to draw the kind of road map you would normally see in an atlas. Why our teacher thought this suitable for nine-year olds I do not know. Although always possessing a bit of a talent for writing, I have never been the greatest artist, my skills stretched to the limit if asked to draw mere stickmen. Needless to say, my map was looking decidedly ropey and my frustration was starting to rise accordingly. As despair began to set in, a familiar piece of music with a distinct oriental flavour wafted over from the television to the dining table where I was sitting. *The Water Margin* had started and my homework woes were forgotten as I quickly moved over to the settee. It is strange how seemingly unremarkable moments like this can stay lodged in your memory for years afterwards. Incidentally, in case any of you were wondering, my older brother helped to complete my homework for me.

The Water Margin was a strange beast. A Japanese television adaptation of one of the four classic novels of Chinese literature, the series was dubbed into English when broadcast here in the UK and featured a narration by Burt Kwouk which was not present in the original production. The scripts often included rather obscure and downright baffling Chinese philosophical sayings and it is telly legend Kwouk's commendably straight delivery of these bizarre quotes which linger in the memory.

When adapting the scripts for British television, writer David Weir paid scant attention to the original plots. How close the British episodes were to their Japanese counterparts is anybody's guess. The actors employed to provide the dubbing were mostly British, leading to varying degrees of success when it came to interpreting the Chinese accent. Can you imagine the same scenario in today's society? A group of British stars adopting Asian accents to dub over the voices of Japanese actors? It just wouldn't happen in the modern world.

Amongst the voice cast for the British version of *The Water Margin* was the wonderful Miriam Margolyes, who was still in the fledgling stages of her career at the time. The cast also included David Collings who, just a short time later, would provide the English-speaking voice of the title character in another wildly popular Japanese import, *Monkey*.

When *The Water Margin* was first broadcast on BBC2 in 1976, it was shown after the nine o'clock watershed. Repeats in later years would air much earlier in the evening, around 6pm. It is these repeat showings that I remember watching as a young lad and the reason I have included the series in this section of the book. Whenever I hear that famous theme tune today, I smile as I recall my awful attempts at drawing that damn road map.

In 1978, from Monday to Friday, my favourite time of day was 17:40pm. As this hallowed time approached each day, I would make sure that my parents had the television tuned to BBC2 for *The Laurel and Hardy Showcase*. This was an umbrella title for a season of Stan Laurel and Oliver Hardy's greatest short films. With the majority of the legendary comedy duo's one-reel comedies running for just twenty minutes, they were perfect for filling the gap between the mind-numbingly dull *Open University* and the admittedly watchable *The Waltons*. Hugely popular with the early evening viewing public, BBC2 continued to show Stan and Ollie's short films on a regular basis for the next four years, always at 17:40pm and always on a weekday evening. In 1982, we got double the laughter as *The Laurel and Hardy Showcase* became *The Laurel and Hardy Double Bill*.

Out of all of the entries in this book, amongst all of the wonderful nostalgic memories, these BBC2 screenings of Laurel and Hardy undoubtedly had the biggest influence on me, both in terms of my viewing habits and the person that I would become. The on-screen Stan and Ollie were two nice guys trying to negotiate their way through life as best as they could. They were unfailingly polite and courteous, as indeed were the real-life Stan and Ollie. As a child, I determined I was going to display the same good manners and, for the most part, I have done just that.

In addition to their influence on me as a person, Stan Laurel and Oliver Hardy were my first comedy heroes and remain extremely important to me today. This is due in many ways to my late father, who would watch these BBC2 screenings with me. Laurel and Hardy were his absolute favourites and, as I laughed

During the Proper Telly era, weekdays at 17:40pm on BBC2 were reserved for the wonderful Laurel and Hardy. (Universal)

alongside him at their on-screen antics, they quickly became my favourites too.

When my father was 70, we had a family party to celebrate. Myself and a very dear friend of mine had formed a guitar/vocal duo at the time and therefore provided part of the entertainment for the party. We included Laurel and Hardy's famous signature song *Trail of the Lonesome Pine* in our set and very quickly the whole room, including my normally shy father, was singing along with us. It was a treasured moment.

Stan Laurel and Oliver Hardy formed the perfect partnership. Stan developed all of their gags and routines and was very much the creative force behind the scenes. Meanwhile, Oliver, or Babe as he was affectionately known off-camera, liked to unwind after filming by playing a relaxing round of golf. He fully trusted Stan's ability as an all-round filmmaker, while Stan was perfectly happy being left to the creative side, understanding that Ollie wasn't as interested in that side of things. Babe liked to concentrate on his work in front of the cameras.

On-screen, they were both magical. Stan's supreme skill as a physical comedian was equal to anything that Charlie Chaplin produced. Oliver Hardy's superbly executed mannerisms, such as the exasperated look to camera and his bashful tie-twiddle, have become legendary and it is often these smaller, more subtle moments that I enjoy the most when watching one of the their films. What always comes across to me when watching Laurel and Hardy is their real-life warmth and obvious affection for each other. I think that is the secret to their long-lasting appeal through a number of generations - genuine warmth and a simple desire to make people laugh.

Amongst my personal favourite Laurel and Hardy shorts are *Helpmates*, which sees Ollie foolishly enlisting the help of Stan to clean up the aftermath of a wild party before his wife returns home; *Blotto*, in which our boys get drunk on liquor during Prohibition, not realising that Ollie's wife has replaced the contents of the bottle with cold tea; *Them Thar Hills*, which sees Stan and Ollie once again the worse for wear for drink after downing water from a well which has had illegal whiskey dumped in it and *Laughing Gravy*, a true classic concerning Stan and Ollie's attempts at concealing the presence of an adorable little dog from their landlord.

Although the BBC very rarely show Laurel and Hardy films these days, at the time of writing Stan and

Ollie can thankfully still be seen on the vintage film channel Talking Pictures TV.

You may think that there is no obvious link between the classic black and white comedy films of Laurel and Hardy and daytime television soap operas from Australia. Well, you are absolutely right - there is no link. So, I'll just move on.

A bastion of Australian TV soap operas, *The Young Doctors* alternated broadcast on the ITV network with that other doyen of Aussie serial drama *Sons and Daughters*. Much like its counterpart, *The Young Doctors* was basically a load of old tosh. However, it was highly addictive tosh.

Debuting in its native Australia on the Nine Network on November 9 1976, the saga of the lives and loves of the medical staff at the fictional Albert Memorial Hospital ran for well over one thousand episodes, finally coming to an end in 1983. At the time, this made *The Young Doctors* the longest-running drama in Australian television history. This record would eventually be broken by a certain soap set in the fictional borough of Erinsborough featuring Kylie Minogue and Jason Donavan.

I was twelve when *The Young Doctors* first appeared on UK screens in 1982. The Central ITV region broadcast the series at 3:45pm each weekday and I can remember sitting down to watch the drama unfold before going upstairs to complete my homework.

For a medical based drama, the series featured very few storylines involving the actual patients of Albert Memorial Hospital. Instead, it was the medical staff taking centre stage. To be perfectly honest, I can't really recall any of the plots with particular clarity today, such was the scatterbrain nature of the writing. I do, however, remember many of the characters.

There was the debonair hospital superintendent Dr Denham, grey-haired surgeon Dr Shaw (who I believe had an affair with Denham's young wife, despite being old enough to be her father), the earnest Dr Graham Steele, the fearsome Sister Scott (played by the prolific Aussie soap legend Cornelia Francis) and gossipy kiosk lady Ada, who seemed to know everything about the goings on in the hospital, despite spending most of her time pouring cups of coffee and dispensing chocolate bars. Joining the cast in 1979 was future *Neighbours* icon Alan Dale. Before taking up residence in Ramsay Street as Jim Robinson, Alan portrayed Dr John Forrest in *The Young Doctors*, sporting a rather startling afro which seemed to develop a life of its own.

The sets might have been basic, the storylines melodramatic and the acting merely functional but *The Young Doctors* was bad television at its best. However, for fast-paced, completely over the top storylines which stretched credulity to the absolute limit and made *The Young Doctors* seem positively pedestrian in comparison, it's hard to beat *Sons and Daughters*.

Here in the UK, we all think of this completely bonkers piece of television as a daytime soap, due to the timeslot it was allocated on the ITV network. However, in its home nation of Australia the series was broadcast at 7pm. Perhaps another reason for us forever linking the show with afternoon drama was the obvious influence of daytime soaps from the USA, *Sons and Daughters* aping many of the plot devices seen in such Stateside shows as *Days of Our Lives* and, in particular, *The Young and the Restless*.

The show's memorable but sickly sweet theme tune promised us '*Sons and daughters, love and laughter, tears and sadness and happiness...*' Well, we certainly got all that, in addition to affairs, divorces, long-lost relatives, shady business dealings, shootings, abortion and even murder.

Undoubtedly, the character which everyone remembers from *Sons and Daughters* is Patricia or, as the British press dubbed her at the time, Pat the Rat. Played with relish by Rowena Wallace, Patricia was one of soap land's most glorious bitches. With her permanently sharpened claws forever embedded in someone's back, Patricia schemed and manipulated her way through life, running roughshod over anybody who dared to get in her way. She was the classic pantomime villain, the devious glint in her eyes simply a prelude to another diabolical plan. I have fond memories of coming home from school to find my mom booing and hissing at the television whenever Patricia came on screen.

Despite the show featuring a plethora of other characters popular in their own right, such as 'Mr Nasty' Wayne, the dependable Beryl and former brothel owner Fiona, it was the wonderfully despicable Pat whom viewers tuned in to see. When Rowena Wallace left *Sons and Daughters* in 1985, the show's producers understandably panicked. They drafted in a number of new villainous female characters in an attempt to fill the void but ratings inevitably began to fall.

In a last ditch effort to keep remaining viewers, the character of Patricia was brought back, albeit played by a different actress. In perhaps the most absurd storyline ever featured in *Sons and Daughters*, and there really was some pretty formidable competition for that honour, Patricia was said to have undergone plastic surgery in South America, before returning to Australia complete with a new identity, looking to exact her revenge on those she deemed had wronged her. Meanwhile, her former lover David Palmer married a Patricia lookalike who had received plastic surgery of her own at the same hospital, the love-struck groom believing her to be the original Patricia. Confused yet? There's more. Series six, which proved to be the final season of *Sons and Daughters,* finally saw actress Rowena Wallace return to the cast, only this time in the role of Patricia's twin-sister Pamela, a sympathetic character destined to feud with bad girl Patricia, who was now called Alison and looked nothing like her twin due to the plastic surgery!

I couldn't very well write a section on after-school television from the seventies and eighties without including the most iconic school-based TV drama of all-time, *Grange Hill.* So popular was this often gritty take on life in a North London comprehensive school, the series ran for an amazing 601 episodes, covering four decades, from 1978 to 2008. With such an impressive longevity, fans of *Grange Hill* cover quite an age range and have quite differing choices when it comes to their favourite characters.

For me, the characters and the plotlines that I recall most vividly are all from the early period of *Grange Hill,* from its very beginning in February 1978 up until approximately 1988 when my interest began to wane as my age increased.

Devised by Phil Redmond, who would go on to create other long-running dramas such as *Brookside* and *Hollyoaks,* the very first episode of *Grange Hill* was broadcast on BBC1 at 5:10pm on Wednesday 8 February 1978. This initial series ran for just nine episodes and was followed in January 1979 with a second series, extended to eighteen episodes in length.

The original roster of pupils in Form 1 Alpha included many students who remain amongst the most fondly recalled by *Grange Hill* aficionados of a certain age. Tucker Jenkins is arguably the most famous *Grange Hill* pupil of them all. So popular was he, the cheeky young pupil even got his own spin-off series, *Tucker's Luck*, which followed the now teenage Tucker and his mate Alan as they struggled to adapt to life as young adults. Actor Todd Carty has enjoyed a very successful career post *Grange Hill*, including long-running roles in *EastEnders* and *The Bill*, but it is the mischievous Tucker for which he is best remembered.

Tucker's best mate at school was Benny Green, an aspiring footballer who played for the school team. Actor Terry Sue-Patt, who portrayed Benny, sadly died in 2015 aged just fifty. Other characters from these early years which had a lasting impact on viewers include Tucker and Benny's friend Alan, the rebellious Suzanne Ross (played by future EastEnder Susan Tully), Trisha Yates, hapless comic foil Pogo Patterson, the romantically linked Stewpot Stewart and Claire Scott and hateful bully Gripper Stebson along with his favourite target, the overweight Roland Browning.

The list of iconic characters residing in the teachers' lounge makes for similarly impressive reading. Who can forget no-nonsense head Mrs McCluskey, hard-nosed PE teacher Mr Baxter and, perhaps most famously of all (maybe should that be infamously), the terrifying Mr Bronson, who gave all school kids of the eighties nightmares, despite the fact he sported a ridiculous wig. The late actor Michael Sheard, who portrayed Mr Bronson with such relish and joyful zeal, would later portray Adolf Hitler on a number of occasions. Many would say Mr Bronson was still the more terrifying.

Over the years, *Grange Hill* courted plenty of controversy with its hard-hitting storylines. Although there was plenty of fun to be had with the hopeless money-making schemes operated by the likes of Pogo and Gonch, it is for the grittier plots which *Grange Hill* is best known.

Racism, bullying and teenage pregnancy all raised their ugly heads during the show's thirty year tenure but there is one storyline which stood head and shoulders above all others in terms of the impact it had on the viewing audience.

During the ninth series in 1986, one of Grange Hill's most popular pupils, Zammo McGuire, became addicted to heroin. The often harrowing storyline ran through the entire ninth series and spilled over into the early part of series ten, seeing the once affable Zammo gradually becoming more distant with his friends and family and resorting to stealing in order to fund his habit. When Roland found Zammo slumped in the corner of a toilet at the back of an amusement arcade, eyes glazed, a piece of heroin-filled foil in his hand, it sent shockwaves across the nation and no doubt resulted in the meltdown of the BBC switchboard.

The brilliant performance of Lee MacDonald as the tormented Zammo rightly won a lot of plaudits, as indeed did the storyline itself. To further the anti-drug message, the pop single *Just Say No,* featuring members of the *Grange Hill* cast, was released in April 1986, peaking at number five in the UK music chart.

Although the inevitable decline in quality which affects all long-running series descended on *Grange*

Hill during the mid-nineties, the show soldiered on until 2008 before the axe finally fell. During its first twelve years in particular, *Grange Hill* produced some of the finest drama and most unforgettable characters in children's television history. Oh, and perhaps the most famous sausage ever seen in a credits sequence too.

A number of children's shows broadcast on a weekday afternoon were educational, broadcasters no doubt hoping that the kids watching were still in learning mode having not long returned from a day at school. Without question, the most famous of these shows was *Blue Peter*. First broadcast on Thursday 16 October 1958, this mainstay of British television is still going today, with an amazing 5000+ episodes in the bank. At the time of writing there have been thirty-seven *Blue Peter* presenters, along with ten dogs, nine cats, five tortoises and two parrots. As the series has been on air for an incredible sixty years, a number of different generations of viewers have grown up with the show, the presenters and pets you most identify with dependent on your age. When I first began watching *Blue Peter,* the classic trio of Valerie Singleton, Peter Purves and John Noakes were at the helm, the iconic Noakes always with faithful dog Shep at his side. The regularly heard cry of "Get down Shep!" was a part of many a childhood. Other presenters I recall with fondness are Lesley Judd, Simon Groom and Peter Duncan, along with golden retriever Goldie and tabby cat Jack.

ITV's answer to *Blue Peter* was *Magpie*. Running from 1968 to 1980, Magpie tried to be a bit more 'hip' than the seemingly staid *Blue Peter*. Despite proving popular, it could never really compete with BBC's flagship afternoon children's show. However, presenters Jenny Hanley and Mick Robertson (he with the hair) remain familiar figures in the memories of seventies schoolkids.

There were plenty of other shows in the *Proper Telly* era which kept us entertained on a weekday afternoon. How many do you remember?

Runaround; *On Safari*; *How*; *Screen Test*; *We Are the Champions*; *John Craven's Newsround*; *Cheggars Plays Pop*; *Crackerjack*; *Clapperboard*; *Huckleberry Finn and his Friends*;

SECRET LEMONADE DRINKER-PROPER ADVERTS

In recent years we have been privileged to witness one of the greatest innovations in the history of mankind - the ability to pause live television. This marvellous, most useful of technological advances is responsible for saving us from hours of mind-numbingly boring and exceedingly irritating advertisements, allowing us to fast-forward x30 through the dross. With many viewers now either pausing their televisions or simply recording programmes to watch at a later time, the number of people actually watching adverts these days must surely have decreased quite dramatically. This would certainly explain why advertising executives seem to put minimum effort into their commercial productions today.

With a few notable exceptions, such as the long-running and very endearing meerkat adverts, most commercials on the box today are instantly forgettable and, in many cases, thoroughly annoying. Back in the *Proper Telly* era however, things were very different.

The fact that many of the advertisements seen on commercial television during the seventies and eighties are still remembered with fondness today is a testament to the marketing genius of advertising executives of the period. A number of these classic TV advertising campaigns were fun to watch and boasted simple but effective slogans and jingles.

Arguably the greatest series of adverts ever seen on British television was that for *Cadbury's Smash*. First appearing on our screens in 1974, the family of metal martians who roared with laughter at the laborious way we humans prepared mashed potato have become iconic figures in British telly history.

One of the most memorable moments in the *Smash* series, when one of the aliens fell over due to uproarious laughter, was actually the result of an accident. The alien puppet toppled over by mistake during filming but the filmmakers decided to keep it in the final edit.

With sales of *Cadbury's Smash* going through the roof due to the success of the commercials, our Martian friends were still promoting the benefits of instant mashed potato in the early part of the next decade, with the slogan 'For Mash get Smash' rightly taking its place in the annals of *Proper Telly* history.

In a similar vein to the *Smash* adverts, albeit this time using living creatures instead of puppets, the *PG Tips* campaign featuring the PG chimps was another hugely successful, long-running series of advertisements. Starring chimpanzees from Twycross Zoo in Leicestershire as the Tipps family, these beloved advertisements sent sales of the *PG Tips* brand soaring and turned the apes into superstars, The commercials saw the chimpanzees dressed in various human guises, the most famous perhaps being the 'Mr Shifter' episode where two chimps try to move a piano downstairs.

The *Tipps Family* campaign actually began way back in 1956 and ran for an amazing forty-six years, an enforced eighteen-month hiatus at the start of the seventies due to pressure from animal rights groups being the only time the chimps were absent from our screens.

Despite the public falling in love with the simian stars of *PG Tips,* the argument against using wild animals in such a way is a very valid one. Although the founder and original owner of Twycross Zoo said that her chimpanzees always enjoyed dressing up in the various human costumes, it has come to light in recent years that the chimps had difficulty interacting with their own species after the advertising campaign ended, as they were more used to human contact. Louis, the male chimp who played the piano mover Mr Shifter, was removed from the acting roster when he reached sexual maturity as his strength and unpredictable behaviour could have posed serious danger to the crew. Although I have many fond memories of watching and laughing at the Tipps chimpanzee family, I am glad that the use of animals for such purposes is no longer tolerated. In fact, I watched a compilation of the PG Tips commercials in question during the writing of this book and, rather than laughing, instead felt sympathy for the chimpanzees. I know that they were highly trained and always treated well but it now feels wrong to see them dressed in such a way.

Speaking of costume, a daredevil action hero clad completely in black set ladies hearts fluttering when he delivered his first box of chocolates in 1968. The *Milk Tray Man* was a James Bond style macho-man who risked life and limb for thirty-four years, all to deliver boxes of Cadbury's Milk Tray to various beautiful women. It was all done undercover of course, with a mysterious calling card left next to the box. If I was him, I wouldn't have bothered scaling mountains, outrunning avalanches or jumping out of helicopters if the lady in question didn't even know who had left her the chocolates in the first place. I'd expect a bit of gratitude in return.

From 1968 to 1984, the *Milk Tray Man* was played by Australian model and actor Gary Myers. Gary was perhaps the most famous of the six Milk Tray men and featured in eleven adverts, performing memorable deeds such as jumping from a moving train and fighting a Great White Shark. All because the lady loves Milk Tray.

As far as chocolate goes, I've always had a liking for Fruit and Nut bars. In the seventies, *Cadbury's Fruit and Nut* was the focus of a television advertising campaign which is still remembered fondly today. As with the other Cadbury's products *Smash* and *Milk Tray*, the *Fruit and Nut* campaign featured a simple but memorable tag line, 'Everyone's a fruit and nut case!" This slogan was also part of the legendary jingle which accompanied each advert. Debonair comedy icon Frank Muir would merrily sing about everyone being a fruit and nut case to the tune of Danse des Mirlitons from Tchaikovsky's *The Nutcracker*. A *Fruit and Nut* advert from 1976 featured dear old Frank punting down a river while treating us to a Noel Coward style rendition of the following lyrics, all to the tune of Danse des Mirlitons –

Everyone's a fruit and nut case
It keeps you going when you toss the caber
Whatever you are doing, punting, canoeing,
It's nutritious and beauticious to judiciously be chewing
Everyone's a fruit and nut case
If only it could help improve my singing
A healthy recreation, what a combination
Cadbury's Fruit and Nut.

They don't write 'em like that anymore.

Adverts for chocolates, sweets and drinks were often memorable. Those people at Cadbury's were at it again with the quite brilliant series of adverts in the early seventies for their *Curly Wurly* bar. Starring comedy legend Terry Scott in his cheeky schoolboy guise, the commercials were set in various locations such as a museum, a ghost train and a farm, each one ending with Scott's schoolboy exclaiming that the *Curly Wurly* 'outchews everything for 3p.'

Moving forward slightly to the early eighties, Cadbury's once again went down the celebrity route by hiring various comedy stars to front the campaign for their new *Wispa* bar. Famous faces featured included Windsor Davies and Don Estelle in character from *It Ain't 'Alf Hot Mum* and Arthur Lowe and John Le Mesurier as Captain Mainwaring and Sergeant Wilson from *Dad's Army*.

One of the most catchy jingles from the seventies was that which accompanied the *Secret Lemonade Drinker* campaign for R Whites Lemonade. One of the most memorable jingles of all-time, the *Secret Lemonade Drinker* song was composed and sung by Ross McManus, the father of Elvis Costello. Elvis himself provided backing vocals for the jingle.

Being a child during the seventies and for the first half of the eighties, the television adverts which would interest me most of course were those for toys and games. I am sure most of us can recall the commercials of our childhood, selling us (or rather our parents) must-have toys and games from the time, such as the *Evel Knievel Stunt Bike* or the latest *Action Man* figure.

I remember these adverts always seemed to feature freckle-faced kids with perfectly combed blonde hair and, unless the product being advertised was gender-specific, it was invariably one boy and one girl. They were always smartly dressed too. How unrealistic was that? As a lad, I cannot ever recall donning my best clothes in order to launch my *Action Man* complete with parachute out of the bedroom window.

Not every toy commercial featured fresh-faced kids however. When Milton Bradley launched their version of the classic game *Hangman* in 1980, they engaged the services of horror film legend Vincent Price. Not only did Price star in the western-themed television advert, he also featured prominently on the front of the game box too. I am sure that not many children at the time would have known who Vincent Price was but it was a very clever way of broadening the game's appeal to include adults too, who enjoyed this type of board game just as much as the kids.

We seventies kids really were lucky. Not only did we get to watch the greatest children's television of all-time and be privy to many wonderful adverts, we also got to play with some of the very best toys and games ever made too. Seeing as we have arrived, in a roundabout way, at the subject of toys and games, let's take a commercial break of our own and take a closer look at some of my personal favourite toys from the *Proper Telly* era.

Evel Knievel Stunt Bike

There can't be many seventies boys who did not, at one time or another, gleefully play with the *Evel Knievel Stunt Bike*. One of the most fondly remembered boys' toys of all-time, it seemed to strike a huge chord with children of the *Proper Telly* era and, even though very much a product of its time, it has never lost its nostalgic appeal to men of a certain age, myself included.

Consisting of an action figure replica of legendary motorcycle stuntman Evel Knievel sat atop one of his famous bikes and a big, clunky red box complete with starter handle, the idea was to set up various ramps and obstacles, either in the garden or on the living room floor, for Evel to spectacularly jump over. The bike was propelled across the floor via a mechanism in the red box. I am sure many of us remember scraping knuckles on the ground as we furiously turned the handle on the red box, which began to rotate the rear wheel of Evel's bike. As cool revving sounds filled the air, a simple press of a button would send our brave biker hurtling across the floor at great speed before hitting the homemade ramp and majestically flying through the air like the most gracious of birds. Well, that's what happened on the television advert at least. In real life, the bike would usually skid sideways across the floor before madly rotating on the spot like a dying fly.

The helmet on the action figure could be taken off and I remember action figure Evel's face not really resembling the real-life daredevil to any real degree. Not that it really mattered to us kids. Much more important was the fact that the head was quite soft and could be squashed between your fingers. This meant that if your Evel was involved in a particularly spectacular crash, you could give his head a quick squeeze and pretend his face had been horribly disfigured in the accident. If you had *Action Man* accessories too, poor old Evel could even spend time in a military medical unit. He would always survive of course, ready to take on another insane challenge, such as jumping over a line of Matchbox cars after traversing Beano annual ramps rested on the corner of your mom's shoeboxes.

The *Evel Knievel Stunt Bike* was pretty simple in both concept and design but the resulting play was absolutely magical to a young boy. We had to use our imagination to come up with ever more elaborate stunts for our daredevil to take on, which piqued our curiosities too. Most importantly, it was just pure fun.

Top Trumps

The concept of *Top Trumps* was incredibly simple but gameplay was devilishly addictive. Dubreq, who manufactured the original *Top Trumps* range, cleverly tapped into the collectables market by releasing a number of different sets for children to collect, all at a price which was affordable to pocket-money conscious kids.

The *Top Trumps* sets each had individual themes, such as sports cars, international footballers, military aircraft or ships. Each card in the set would feature a number of statistics which players would compare with that of their opponents. If the particular statistic you had chosen was better than that of your opponent, you would win their card. In the case of a draw, the cards would be placed in the middle of the table ready for a rollover. The first player to have all of the game cards in their possession would be declared the winner.

Although *Top Trumps* was obviously designed as a game for at least two people, it could often be equally as interesting to flick through the cards by yourself, soaking up the various snippets of information listed. To some, this may sound like the height of boredom and even perhaps a bit geeky. However, I believe that my love of trivia, lists and statistics all came from *Top Trumps*. The range of subjects available in the *Top Trumps* collection was vast, so you could really

The re-release version of the classic Horror Pack.
(Winning Moves)

broaden your knowledge on a myriad of subjects, such as sport, transport, animals and even fictional horror characters.

The aforementioned horror set was one which I remember most vividly. Each card in the pack featured an artist's depiction of a different horrifying creature. The artwork was what made the *Top Trumps Horror Pack* an essential purchase for boys of a certain age. Drawn in a comic book style, with plenty of blood and gore thrown in, the horror set was, unsurprisingly, the most popular *Top Trumps* pack in the school playground. Obviously the statistics for each creature were pure fantasy, unlike the vast majority of other *Top Trumps* sets which were hard fact. I don't think anyone could ever prove, beyond any reasonable doubt, that The Slime Creature possessed a physical strength greater than that of The Living Skull or that Wolfman's overall horror rating was vastly inferior to that attributed to Mistress Vampire. Looking through each card in the *Horror Pack* while writing this book, I found it quite amazing how many of the creature depictions I remember so vividly from those nostalgic days of my youth. The Fire Demon still looks like Jeff Lynne from ELO, while the character of Dr Syn so closely resembles Christopher Lee as Fu Manchu I'm amazed there were no copyright issues at the time. Incidentally, the actual *Top Trumps* Fu Manchu card was based on the features of Boris Karloff, although Christopher Lee did make another appearance in the form of Dracula, both in the set and on the front of the box. The Count was one of the strongest cards to have in your hand if I remember correctly.

Of course, there was much more to *Top Trumps* than just a horror set. The overall number of packs available was vast and I had a decent number of them in my own collection. Packs I remember playing include *Sports Cars, Tanks, Super Cars, Grand Prix Cars, Dragsters, International Footballers* and *Superbikes*.

In 1999, Winning Moves relaunched the *Top Trumps* brand to great acclaim and millions of packs are still sold to eager children every day.

Action Man

Arguably the greatest boys toy ever produced. Surely every boy of the seventies, or indeed eighties, had at least one *Action Man* in their toy collection. I know I did. In fact, I had several.

The all-conquering British hero *Action Man* can actually trace his roots to the USA. The action figure *GI Joe* was a huge success when launched in the United States in 1964, despite some initial fears that the toy would be a flop, as it was, essentially, a 'doll' for boys. These fears would not be realised however and so, in an effort to replicate that success in Britain, manufacturer Palitoy released *Action Man* in 1966, gradually steering their version away from its US counterpart and adding a unique sense of Britishness to it.

Ask any seventies lad a physical characteristic that they remember *Action* Man possessing and you will more than likely receive the answer 'fuzzy hair'. This was a design update first seen in 1970, replacing the frankly rubbish painted hair with more realistic and tougher looking flock hair. Some figures even had that awesome flock hair look enhanced still further by the addition of a beard, again in that glorious fuzzy style. I loved the bearded *Action Man*, although I am not sure my elder brother felt the same way. He treated one of his bearded figures to a shave, using our dad's razor to give the heroic soldier a smoother look. It didn't really work. The newly shaven *Action Man* looked like he had been involved in an horrific accident, his face resembling a very badly peeled potato.

Another feature added to *Action Man* in the early seventies was the grip hand. Previously, the figures had rather ineffectual hard plastic hands which were totally immobile. The new grip feature meant *Action Man* could now brandish all manner of weapons with ease. The one downside to grip hands was the difficulty often encountered when trying to dress your figure in new clothes. The grip hand would regularly get caught in the sleeves of the outfit, causing much annoyance to impatient boys everywhere. This small gripe was solved with the release of a mini plastic thimble which slotted over *Action Man's* hands, making the adorning of a new outfit a doddle. Genius!

There were a great number of outfits available for *Action Man*. In addition to a myriad of various military uniforms, you could also turn your hero into an astronaut, deep sea diver, footballer, life guard, jungle explorer or a polar explorer.

Other seventies innovations for *Action Man* included the legendary Eagle Eyes in 1976, which saw our hero's eyes swivel from left to right via a lever on the back of his neck and also the spectacular addition of blue underpants in 1979.

For many of us, the most exciting aspect of playing with *Action Man* was the quite brilliant range of accessories available. The bigger your collection of *Action Man* accessories, the higher your standing amongst your peers. Each accessory was well constructed and added so much enjoyment to play, particularly the vehicles. I remember having the helicopter, the military jeep and, perhaps best of all, the tank. I'm pretty sure I had a horse too. With the addition of a jungle boat, you could even turn your bath into a tropical river teeming with untold dangers.

In addition to vehicles, you could also get fantastic items such as the field radio, featuring mini coloured discs that, once popped into the radio pack, would play various realistic messages. The discs were coloured blue, red, yellow and clear. Nothing could quite match the excitement of hearing an official-sounding voice coming from your radio pack requesting air support or commanding you to 'commence firing'. Like many boys, I also had the parachute kit and would regularly send various members of my *Action Man* squad on missions from my bedroom fortress base, where the only way to exit was via the window, parachuting down into the jungle (make that garden) below.

Since production ceased in the mid-eighties, *Action Man* has made a number of comebacks, usually in the guise of special anniversary editions. Sadly, it seems that today's more politically correct, sensitive society has deemed that a rough, tough military action figure is no longer a suitable toy for boys to play with.

Six Million Dollar Man

Although *Action Man* was the daddy of action figures, there are many others from the seventies and eighties which have now attained classic status. A number of them were based on popular television series of the time.

Arguably the most famous of these television spin-off figures was the *Six Million Dollar Man*. Starring Lee Majors as Colonel Steve Austin, the *Six Million Dollar Man* TV series debuted in the United States in 1974 and ran for five seasons. The premise saw former astronaut Austin undergo experimental bodily repair procedures after being involved in a major accident. His right arm and both of his legs have bionic implants inserted, giving him superhuman strength and allowing him to run at incredible speed. His left eye is fitted with a zoom lens and infrared functions. With such amazing capabilities, Austin is soon employed as an agent for a secret government organisation.

The Six Million Dollar Man series is perhaps most fondly remembered today for the memorable opening title sequence, featuring that iconic theme music playing over footage of Austin undergoing the bionic procedures, while a voiceover confidently states, "We can rebuild him. We have the technology."

With the show very quickly assembling a huge fan base, it was perhaps inevitable that a range of merchandise would follow. In 1975, US toy manufacturer Kenner released a range of action figures to complement the series. Obviously, the most popular figure, by far, was Steve Austin himself. Like me, millions of seventies kids will have fond memories of looking through a hole in the back of Austin's head in order to see out of his bionic eye and pressing a lever on his back to make him lift an engine block with his bionic right arm. One of the most amazing features of the *Six Million Dollar Man* action figure was the rollback rubber skin on his arm and legs. Pulling this skin back allowed you to see the bionic circuitry underneath. To a young boy, this was just incredible. They certainly don't make them like that anymore.

A Selection of Favourite Board Games

Despite the modern-day presence of PlayStation and Xbox and undeterred by the dominance of smartphones, the humble board game refuses to lie down and become a mere distant memory. Although sales of board games are not at the level they were back in the *Proper Telly* era, they still shift enough units to persuade manufacturers to keep producing them.

This is, of course, great news for fans of all things retro. I loved playing board games as a kid and I still enjoy the odd dabble today. There's nothing quite like a good old-fashioned board game for bringing family and friends together. Some may argue that the advent of online gaming allows you to play with more people at the same time than ever before, people that don't even have to be beside you in the room. However, from the evidence I have seen, online gaming exists mainly to give gaming obsessives the opportunity to shout abuse at each other over sweaty headsets, as they try to cut their opponents to ribbons on a WWII battlefield.

Board games have a proper physical presence that adds to the excitement of playing. The board laid out in front of you, the playing pieces in position, the dice ready to throw and the instructions read but still not understood by everyone...this is what playing games is all about!

I had a number of favourite board games as a kid, many of which I dearly wish I still owned today. Unfortunately, as I advanced into my teenage years, I decided to sell most of my collection, a decision I deeply regret. A number of the games I sold are worth quite a bit of money now, although the market isn't quite as buoyant as it was a couple of years ago. Mind you, it isn't just the value that bothers me. It is the fact that a part of my childhood disappeared as soon as I sold those games over thirty years ago. I am sorely tempted to raid marketplaces such as eBay in order to buy back some of the classic games of my childhood.

I would love to recapture the spirit of those childhood days by once again playing such absolute gems as *Game of Dracula*. Released by industry veterans Waddington's in 1977, the aim of *Game of Dracula* was to escape from Dracula's castle while being chased by the fiendish Count himself. If you were caught by Dracula or one of his vampires, their figures would slot over your playing piece, completely engulfing you. A great little innovation I remember from *Game of Dracula* was the inclusion of a green vampire bat mask. The first player to be bitten in the game would have to don the cardboard mask and then hunt down the other players via the green vampire playing piece. There was also a blue vampire piece, while the plastic figure of Dracula was red.

Officially licenced merchandise based on films and television programmes has always been a great money-spinner for manufacturers and usually a splendid source of fun and collectability for consumers. Back in the seventies, the ITV sitcom *On The Buses* was hugely popular, with three spin-off films also pulling in the crowds at cinemas. There was even an *On the Buses* board game. Released in 1973, the box featured some wonderfully drawn cartoon caricatures of Stan, Jack and Inspector Blakey. The aim of the game was to drive your bus around the board, collecting passengers from bus stops along the way, all the while trying to avoid the wrath of Blakey.

The first person to get three passengers back to the depot was declared the winner. I remember the game including four plastic buses, coloured red, green, blue and brown and also a number of plastic bus stops and little plastic passengers which stood in the top of your bus playing piece.

I remember having hours of fun playing this.

Other board games of the seventies and eighties based on TV shows included *The Dukes of Hazzard Game*, *It's a Knockout*, *Kojak* and *Mork & Mindy*.

Although not officially based on the Colditz television series of the early seventies, the *Escape from Colditz* board game always seemed to be linked to its TV cousin. First released in 1973, I remember *Escape from Colditz* being incredibly complicated, with games sometimes taking up to three hours to complete. One player would take on the role of a German security officer while the rest of the players would be one of a differing number of nationalities trying to get their prisoners out of the infamous Colditz Castle. The escapees would first have to assemble a complete escape kit before attempting to traverse their chosen escape route. I can remember playing *Escape from Colditz* with my elder brother and his mates, who were all seven years older than me. I played the German security officer. As I was only about nine at the time and my brother and his mates were sixteen, they understood the complexities of the game far better than I did, leading to Colditz being totally devoid of prisoners at the end of the game!

The superb artwork on the front of the box featured a swastika next to the title when *Escape from Colditz* was first released. This would never happen today of course and later editions of the game saw the swastika replaced by an Imperial Eagle.

There were lots of other games I enjoyed playing back in the seventies and early eighties which weren't actually board games but which still fit nicely into that category. One such game was *Guess Who?* Such a simple premise to this one but hours of fun were guaranteed. With each player having a board containing flip-up stands picturing different characters, the idea was to try to guess which of those characters your opponent had on their main card by asking 'yes' or 'no' type questions. You would then eliminate the characters on your board by flipping them flat. The first person to guess correctly was the winner. *Guess Who?* is one of those timeless games that can be enjoyed by both kids and adults alike. I say that in the present tense because the game is still being produced today such is its popularity, although I believe that the characters are now different. The original characters were by far the best and had a strangely enduring appeal. Who could forget Bernard, the sour-faced Homburg-wearing grump with a distinctly Russian vibe? How about the rotund Bill, winner of the Man Who Most Closely Resembles a Boiled Egg award? Let's not forget the positively dashing Charles, he of the drooping blonde moustache and Swedish porn star looks, or Claire, the original blueprint for Hyacinth Bouquet. These characters, along with the likes of George, Frans, Anita and Eric are on permanent display in the childhood gallery of my memory.

Many of the games from the *Proper Telly* era featured deceptively simple gameplay which was nevertheless highly addictive. Another enduring classic, *Kerplunk* involved the strategic removal of plastic straws from an upright tube, all the while trying not to disturb the mound of marbles which sat precariously atop the straw network. Simple but fun.

In a similar vein to the legendary *Buckaroo* and based on the classic Steven Spielberg film, the *Jaws* game saw players using hooks to remove various items from the mouth the mighty Great White Shark. As the number of items decreased, so the equilibrium altered, inevitably leading to the powerful jaws snapping shut and the game ending.

Another game requiring a steady hand was *Operation*. Undoubtedly one of the most popular and well-known games of all-time, *Operation* was first released by MB way back in 1965. Over fifty years later, it is still in production. Over the years, millions of kids (and indeed adults) have knotted their brows in deep concentration as they try to successfully remove apples from throats, butterflies from stomachs, buckets from knees and slices of bread from bread baskets. Don't touch the sides though or your patient's big red nose is going to start flashing.

With so many other great games in the retro toy loft, such as *Battleship, Tank Command, Rebound, Frustration, Connect Four, Downfall, Mouse Trap, Bermuda Triangle* and *The Fastest Gun*, I could easily fill another chapter on this subject but it's time to get back to more great telly memories.

THE HAIR OF DICKIE DAVIES – PROPER SPORT

If there is one constant in the television schedules, one thing which steadfastly refuses to leave our screens, it is sport. The enthralling drama and sheer theatre of sport has been a part of our viewing lives for over eighty years. Incredibly, the very first television broadcast of a live sporting event occurred way back in 1937. The occasion was Wimbledon and the match shown featured British legend Bunny Austin going up against Irishman George Lyttleton-Rogers in the first round.

My first strong memory of watching sport on television was the final of the football World Cup in 1978. I remember lying on the floor, looking up at the television completely agog at the incredible array of colour on show, as fans of host nation Argentina turned the stadium for the final against the Netherlands into a truly dazzling display of streamers, confetti and flags. Already an impressive facility, the River Plate Stadium in Buenos Aires took on a whole new air of magnificence that night, the magical sight complemented by the unbelievably loud roar of the home fans. Writing this forty years later, I honestly cannot recall any football game since that has managed to equal the electric atmosphere that pervaded the stadium in the Argentine capital that night.

The main man for Argentina, as they beat the Netherlands 3-1 after extra time to lift their first

World Cup, was Mario Kempes. With his long locks flowing behind him as he raced across the pitch celebrating each of his two goals, Kempes looked every inch the dashing seventies footballing hero. The crowd noise after each of Argentina's goals was unlike anything I had heard before or since. In addition to Kempes, the victorious Argentine team also included future legends such as captain Daniel Passarella and Spurs favourite Ossie Ardiles. The unlucky Dutch side had to be content with runners-up medals for the second World Cup in a row, having lost to West Germany in the 1974 final.

As I was just eight years old at the time of the 1978 final, I was able to enjoy the game for the spectacle that it was, my young mind untainted by thoughts of the political situation in Argentina at the time or the overblown histrionics just before kick-off which saw the Argentine team come on to the pitch late and the game almost abandoned due to arguments over the legality of a plaster cast worn on the arm of Dutch winger Rene van de Kerkhof.

Four years later, the 1982 World Cup in Spain featured the greatest footballing side I have ever been privileged to witness. The title of 'Greatest Ever International Football Team' is invariably bestowed upon the magnificent Brazil squad of 1970 and rightly so. With players such as Pele, Rivelino, Jairzinho, Gerson, Tostao and Carlos Alberto in the side, there can be little debate. However, as I was only a few months old at the time, I can't include this Brazil squad as the greatest I have personally seen, as I was still gurgling in my cot as they strutted their stuff. Instead, my choice for greatest side is the 1982 incarnation of Brazil

Mario Kempes celebrates scoring for Argentina during the 1978 World Cup final. (Image: Olga Popova/Shutterstock)

Still regarded today as the best team not to win the tournament, the 1982 Brazil side was full of immense skill and incredible attacking flair. They played the kind of football with which Brazil has always been associated. They were the musketeers of the footballing world – dashing, daring and beguiling. Captain Socrates, highly skilled and extremely influential, was one of my childhood footballing heroes. Also in that squad were legends such as Zico, Junior, Falcao and Eder. Each game they played, I watched in awe as they took other teams apart with exhilarating abandon. However, their love of attack was to be their undoing. Needing just a draw against Italy to advance from the second group stage and into the semi-finals, Brazil refused to compromise their attacking nature. With the score at 2-2 and just over twenty minutes to go, they continued to attack. Italy took advantage of their opponents reluctance to

Italy vs Brazil 1982 was one of the most famous World Cup games in history. (Image: Sergey Kohl/Shutterstock)

defend and scored in the 74th minute to seal a memorable 3-2 victory. Italy went on to win the tournament with top-scoring striker Paolo Rossi becoming a national hero.

Football commentators in the *Proper Telly* era were of a different class to today's rather anonymous bunch. At the BBC, the one and only David Coleman added a sense of occasion to many seventies matches. The BBC line-up also included the likes of Barry Davies and the inimitable John Motson. Meanwhile, over on ITV, the soothing tones of Hugh Johns were always a highlight, as was the comforting, reassuring presence of Brian Moore.

The voices of all of the above were a firm part of my childhood watching sport on television. Many of the great sports commentators had instantly recognisable voices and individual vocal traits that became truly iconic. The legendary Dan Maskell, with his well-known catchphrase 'Oh, I say!' was the voice of tennis for over forty years. In a similar vein, 'Whispering'

Ted Lowe was undoubtedly the voice of snooker. Sadly, the only survivor from this golden age, who still commentates regularly on his chosen sport at time of writing, is golf's Peter Allis, at the grand age of eighty-seven no less.

Back on the subject of football, the FA Cup final was a momentous occasion during the seventies and eighties. Today, the importance of this grand old competition has diminished substantially, to the extent that kick-off time has moved from the traditional 3pm to 5pm. That would have been considered tantamount to treason when I was young.

The Saturday of the FA Cup final was always a day for doing absolutely nothing but watch telly. The build-up to the game itself would start first thing in the morning, so you would always make sure you were up in plenty of time to start watching while munching on a bowl of Frosties. The only decision you had to make on the day was whether to watch the match on BBC or ITV. As ITV usually had the wonderful Brian Moore in the commentary box, I would normally view the game itself on the commercial channel, then switch to BBC for the duration of half-time in order to avoid the adverts.

Another great sporting memory of mine is watching the clashes between Steve Ovett and Sebastian Coe at the 1980 Summer Olympics in Moscow. Once again, as I was still young, it was the highly anticipated showdown between the two middle distance greats which held my attention, rather than the famous boycott of the games led by the United States and supported by many other countries, in response to the invasion of Afghanistan by the USSR.

Sebastian Coe and Steve Ovett contested one of the all-time great sporting rivalries over the course of their respective careers. On the track, they regularly swopped world records in what was essentially a supreme game of one-upmanship. Between them, they dominated the world of middle distance athletics. Undoubtedly, another contributing factor to their white-hot rivalry was the press's obsession with their differing backgrounds and personalities. Ovett was seen to represent the working man while Coe was portrayed as the upper-class boy with the privileged background. In true British press style, most of this was greatly exaggerated but it certainly added fuel to their already burning rivalry.

In the lead up to the Olympics, Sebastian Coe was installed as the favourite for the 800m while Steve Ovett was much fancied in the 1500m, having been unbeaten over the distance for three years. The 800m Olympic final was the first to be run. Amazingly, this was only the second time the two British athletes had raced against each other. This made the clash all the more mouth-watering. I remember that, at the time, it seemed liked the whole nation had come to a standstill to watch these two world-class runners go head to head. My main memories of watching the race on the BBC are of the no-nonsense Ovett barging his way through the field to eventually take the gold and the legendary David Coleman providing another iconic piece of commentary. As the athletes hit the back straight on the final lap he declared of Ovett, "Those blue eyes are like chips of ice!"

With just a silver medal to show from his 800m outing, Sebastian Coe had all of the pressure on him as the 1500m final rolled around. He had been beaten by his bitter rival in his favoured event and now had to regroup to take on Ovett once again, only this time over a distance in which the newly crowned 800m champion had been unbeaten for years. Also in the line-up for the 1500m final was a certain Steve Cram, just nineteen years of age at the time. I remember Cram's unruly mass of curly blonde hair made him look about seven feet tall. In a reversal of fortune from their first clash, it was Coe who sprinted home for the gold this time, David Coleman excited cry of, "Could this be Ovett's first defeat? Ovett is in trouble!" adding to the drama. With Coe grabbing gold, Ovett had to settle for just the bronze this time.

The year 1980 was a vintage one as far as memorable sporting moments are concerned. In addition to the clash of the middle-distance giants at the Moscow Olympics, the World Snooker final from the Crucible Theatre, Sheffield provided drama both on and off the table.

Cliff Thorburn, 1980 World Snooker champion and my favourite player. (Photo: David Fowler/Shutterstock)

I have been a big follower of snooker ever since I was a young lad, no doubt influenced by my father who was also a fan of the game. The climax of the 1980 World Snooker Championship was the first final of which I have vivid memories of watching. It was a bit of a grudge match between the mercurial Alex Higgins and the steely Canadian Cliff Thorburn, my personal favourite player. Although some weren't fans of Thorburn's slower, more measured play, I admired his grit, tenacity and sheer will to win. The Grinder was as tough as nails on the green baize but a lover of life off it, one of his other nicknames being Champagne Cliff.

The match was a Crucible classic, a true clash of styles and personalities. Higgins was in total control of the game and so decided to play to the crowd. This almost reckless abandon by the Irishman simply spurred Thorburn on and he began to reel in Higgins frame by frame. The ice-cool Canadian eventually emerged triumphant by 18 frames to 16 to become the first ever overseas world snooker champion.

However, it was not just the drama on the table for which the 1980 final is famous. Over one hundred and fifty miles away in South Kensington, London, the six-day siege of the Iranian Embassy by Arab terrorists was about to come to a dramatic conclusion. As the two snooker rivals battled away on the green baize, the BBC interrupted proceedings with a newsflash. Viewers were taken to live footage from the Embassy as the SAS dramatically stormed the building. Black-clad figures abseiled from the roof to various balconies below. A charge was laid in front of one of the windows and then a sudden, huge explosion rang out, plumes of smoke permeating the air as the SAS made their way inside.

This must rank as one of the most incredible pieces of live footage ever broadcast on British television. It is a moment which will never be forgotten by those who viewed it. Thankfully the operation was a success, otherwise it would have been remembered for very different, more sobering, reasons.

Incredibly, the BBC received a large amount of complaints from viewers over their coverage of the event, stating that their enjoyment of the snooker had been ruined by the broadcast of the siege. At the time some blissfully unaware viewers believed that the BBC had switched to coverage of a film.

Growing up, Saturday was the designated day for sport on television. To some extent, this is still the case today but, without the likes of *Grandstand* and *World of Sport,* it doesn't seem quite the same.

The BBC's flagship sports show for nearly fifty years, *Grandstand* was first broadcast on October 11 1958. Despite its longevity, the legendary sports magazine programme only ever featured five main presenters. The first was Peter Dimmock, who only fronted two shows before being replaced by that man David Coleman again. After ten years at the helm, Coleman left and was replaced by Frank Bough who remained the show's anchor for an impressive fifteen years. In 1983, the smooth, unflappable and immensely likeable Des Lynam took charge, until Steve Ryder became the last regular presenter in 1993.

Just as everyone has their own *Doctor Who,* dependent on what year you were born, so too we all have our own *Grandstand* presenters. Mine were Frank Bough and Des Lynam. Although he normally wore the de rigueur suit and tie when presenting *Grandstand,* I will always associate Bough with comfy slacks and sensible pullovers due to his time presenting *BBC Breakfast Time.* On April 1 1989, Des Lynam was totally unfazed when a fight broke out amongst the newsroom staff who were always in view behind the main presenter. This was of course later revealed to be an April Fool's Day joke.

With smartphones and the internet, it is now easier than ever to keep up with all of the latest happenings in every sporting event. I do, however, still get a little misty eyed at the memory of the good old *Grandstand* vidiprinter typing out the latest football results as they came in, the score gradually revealed at the bottom of the screen. It made it seem all the more exciting as the result of the match involving your favourite team was typed up as you watched.

Over on ITV, sports fans had to wait seven years before the commercial network decided they needed a show of their own to compete against *Grandstand.* Cut from the same mould as its elder BBC rival, *World of Sport* made its debut on January 2 1965. Genial Irishman Eamonn Andrews was the new show's first anchor, a position he held for three years. In 1968, a new presenter took the reins, a man with a moustache and a truly hypnotic grey-streaked quiff who would become legendary amongst TV sports fans. That man was the one and only Dickie Davies and he would remain the show's main anchor until the final edition in 1985.

Davies was a calm and classy presenter, almost a prototype for Des Lynam really. If he had been an actor, you could see Dickie taking on the kind of roles normally reserved for Leslie Phillips or Terry-Thomas. Over the years, the grey streak in his otherwise dark hair became almost hypnotic. It was impossible not to be transfixed as it seemed to move and grow ever more luxuriant each week.

During the seventies, the opening titles of the show featured a plane trailing the words *World of Sport* behind it, as the famous theme tune played over a compilation of sporting clips. What an array of sport there was too. As the BBC owned the rights to the majority of major sporting events, ITV interspersed coverage of mainstream sports such as football and horse racing with the likes of stock car racing, fishing and log rolling. We even got to see dogs catching Frisbees. Amongst the weird and wonderful menagerie of minority sports from around the globe, *World of Sport* had regular features which were broadcast each and every week. The show usually opened with *On the Ball*, a round-up of the week's football action, initially presented by Brian Moore and then by Ian St John and Jimmy Greaves. So popular were the footballing double act, they even got their own show, *Saint and Greavsie*, after *World of Sport* was cancelled. The mid-point of the five hour show was always taken over by horse racing. This was the point when I, along with many other young people across the country, began to grow ever more restless, especially after switching over to *Grandstand* to find they were showing horse racing too. Snooze.

The seemingly interminable horse racing coverage would finally come to an end at 4pm. My excitement would always rise at this point as it was now time for *World of Sport's* most cherished feature – the wrestling. With dear old Kent Walton in the commentary box, we would be whisked off to a dusty town hall in Darlington or Wigan for the latest wrestling action. *World of Sport* wrestling is one of the most cherished memories of my telly-watching childhood. With the referee's count of 'one-aaa, two-aaa, three-aaa' hanging in the air, my mom would gradually become more and more agitated at the on-screen antics of the wrestling bad guys. What a memorable collection of characters those wrestlers were too; the super heavyweight perennial rivals Big Daddy and Giant Haystacks, supremely villainous Mick McManus, the sneaky Jim Breaks, masked warrior Kendo Nagasaki, the eccentric Catweazle, the powerful Pat Roach and athletic good guy Steve Grey.

Birmingham-born Pat Roach had already branched out into the world of acting back at the start of the seventies when he landed an uncredited role as a bouncer in Stanley Kubrick's *A Clockwork Orange*. With many more film appearances over the ensuing decade, including *Raiders of the Lost Ark*, gentle giant Roach became a familiar face to non-wrestling fans too. In 1982, when filming started on a new comedy drama series set in Germany, Pat Roach was the only member of the main cast to be known to the general public. That series was *Auf Wiedersehen Pet*.

Written by the legendary partnership of Dick Clement and Ian La Frenais, *Auf Wiedersehen Pet* concerned a group of working men who, with employment hard to come by in England, travel to Germany in order to find paid work on a building site. The first episode debuted quietly on ITV on Friday 11 November 1983 but would quickly strike a chord with viewers familiar with the plight of the main characters. The scripts were wonderfully written, the situations relevant and the characters beautifully realised by a talented cast who would not remain unknown for long. The likes of Tim Healey, Jimmy Nail, Kevin Whately and Timothy Spall would go on to become some of the most familiar faces on British television. Back in the wrestling ring, the formerly villainous Pat Roach found the crowds beginning to cheer for him, no doubt due to his gentle performance as burly brickie Bomber in *Auf Wiedersehen Pet*.

When the popularity of the glitzy, deliberately over the top World Wrestling Federation spread from the USA to the rest of the world, the traditional wrestling action seen on *World of Sport* began to look archaic and slow. Although coverage of British wrestling would actually outlive its parent programme *World of Sport* by three years, the writing was on the wall. When ITV finally cancelled wrestling in 1988, a Saturday afternoon viewing tradition that stretched back over twenty years sadly came to an end. Such was the enormity of the decision to wipe wrestling from the ITV schedules, the story was featured on the evening news.

Although *Grandstand* and *World of Sport* were the mainstays of British television sports coverage, there is one show which, for me, epitomises *Proper Telly* sport more than any other. If I ever hear the theme tune to this show today, I immediately picture football star Kevin Keegan suffering a nasty fall from a bicycle or Brian Jacks furiously pounding out squat thrusts like his life depended on it. I am, of course, referring to *Superstars*.

The premise to *Superstars* saw competitors from a variety of sports take part in a multi-event competition involving events such as cycling, swimming, running, football skills and, most memorably of all, the gym tests.

Originating in the USA in early 1973, the BBC decided to make their own version of *Superstars* just a few months later. Presented by sports broadcast legend David Vine, the very first UK competition was broadcast on New Year's Eve 1973. The infamous gym test was in the line-up of events right from the very start. Devised by commentator and athletics coach Ron Pickering, the initial gym test comprised circuit running, medicine ball throws and the famous bar dips and squat thrusts. Former Olympic 400m hurdles champion David Hemery was the first *Superstars* champion, beating off competition from the likes of Bobby Moore, Joe Bugner and Tony Jacklin.

As the seventies progressed, in addition to *UK Superstars*, a European and a World event were added to the calendar. It was while competing in the 1976 *European Superstars* that football star Kevin Keegan suffered that famous fall from his bike, receiving some extremely painful looking abrasions to his arm and back. Ever the determined competitor, Keegan clambered back on to his bike as the race was re-run, a race which he went on to win.

Of all the great competitors to have taken part in *Superstars*, one name stands out from the rest – Brian Jacks. A former Olympic judo star, Jacks was a competitive animal on *Superstars*, particularly when it came to the gym tests. His great upper body strength helped him to an amazing world record of one hundred parallel bar dips in sixty seconds. Jacks also set a formidable personal best of one hundred and eighteen squat thrusts.

The formidable Jacks won two *UK Superstars* titles, as well as a European championship and the *International Superstars* event in 1980. By this time, *Superstars* was gaining in excess of ten million viewers and the former judo man had become a household name. As the eighties dawned, a new champion took on the Jacks mantle of dominant Superstar, Brian Hooper. Pole vaulter Hooper won two UK titles and was 1982 World Champion. However, the glory days of *Superstars* were over by this point. The concept seemed to fit the seventies decade more comfortably and, by the mid-eighties, the series just didn't seem the same.

In terms of the variety of televised sport on offer during the *Proper Telly* days, there wasn't a great deal which originated from America. The likes of basketball and American football did not enjoy a great deal of air time here until the nineties, when sport from the USA experienced a surge in popularity on these shores.

Despite seventies and eighties telly in the UK being light on US sport, we were spoilt for choice in terms of imported American series, a favourite few which I will recall next.

I PITY THE FOOL - PROPER TELLY
USA

The majority of American television series I remember from my childhood and teenage years had one thing in common. They were all fun to watch. Even the high-quality, more serious dramas such as the magnificent *Hill St Blues* possessed addictive qualities that made them as entertaining to watch as they were compelling.

US telly imports of the seventies were usually of the big-city cop variety or instead fantasy action adventures which spawned reams of merchandise, cue *The Six Million Dollar Man*. As the eighties progressed, my favourite American shows were either bursting with over the top action, such as *The A-Team*, awash with glamorous scheming (take a bow, *Dallas*) or filled with laughter (*Cheers* etc.).

The original 1968 *Planet of the Apes* big-screen adventure, based on the novel by Pierre Boulle and starring Charlton Heston, has stood the test of time and remains one of the greatest science-fiction films ever made. If by some chance you have never seen this genre classic, then I will not spoil the ending for you, suffice to say that the iconic final scene retains as much power today as it did at the time of initial release.

Such was the success of the film at the box-office, an inevitable production line of sequels followed during the seventies, the quality declining somewhat with each subsequent release. However, each of the Apes films managed to maintain that all-important fun factor.

All five of the films in the *Planet of the Apes* franchise came along before the television series first aired in 1974, although the idea for a TV adaptation had first been discussed back in 1971. With production efforts concentrated on the making of the films, the small-screen version was put on the back-burner until the CBS network broadcast each of the first three Apes movies in 1973, garnering excellent ratings in the process. It then became a given that a television series would follow.

The first episode of *Planet of the Apes* aired on CBS in the United States on Friday 13 September 1974. In the UK, the series was broadcast on a slight delay, debuting on the ITV network a month later on Sunday 13 October 1974

One of the main things I remember about the TV version of *Planet of the Apes* was the superb opening credits sequence. With the dramatic theme music pounding along in the background, the titles showed how the two human astronauts crash landed on Earth in the far distant future, an Earth that was now controlled by highly intelligent apes. The end of the credit sequence featured an image that has remained with me ever since, a truly magnificent shot of one of the gorilla soldiers on horseback, his right arm stretched high above his head, rifle in hand, fading to silhouette as the still powerful sun sets behind him. As a kid, it was one of the greatest things I had ever seen. Mind you, what young boy wouldn't be completely gripped by the sight of an armed and dangerous anthropomorphic gorilla riding a horse?

It's a shame really that the series itself didn't quite live up to that great opening title sequence. While still being fairly enjoyable, the small-screen version couldn't capture the wonder and zest of its big-screen cousins, one of the main criticisms levelled against it being that the apes themselves weren't featured enough.

The biggest plus for the TV series was having the marvellous Roddy McDowall in the main cast. London-born Roddy was exemplary at playing friendly eccentrics and had been the true star of the *Planet of the Apes* film franchise. He gave a magnificent performance as the chimpanzee Cornelius in the original big-screen outing and appeared in three of the four sequels. In the television series he played pretty much the same character, a chimpanzee sympathetic to the plight of the humans, although here his name was changed to Galen.

With a new Apes franchise wowing cinema audiences in recent years, don't be surprised if a blockbuster television series follows. There has been no word of a new TV outing for our ape friends at time of writing but I can see it happening.

If there was one thing that the makers of American television series could do really well during the *Proper Telly* era, it was creating a superb opening credits sequence. The opening titles are incredibly important in drawing viewers in to a show, hooking us right from the start. A good sequence should make us aware of what to expect from a series, let us in on a few background story details, while leaving some important questions left unanswered. As viewers, we should be left wanting more.

The passage of time has seen many of the truly great opening title sequences become even more iconic than the shows themselves. Many of the nostalgic discussions I have had with friends concerning television shows from the past have begun with the conversation centred on the opening titles, interspersed with various renditions of the theme tunes of course.

It is only natural that, of all the various elements which combine to make a memorable television show, it is the title sequences that stand out most clearly in the nostalgic mist. The old adage of first impressions being lasting impressions certainly rings true. Every time we watched our favourite shows, we obviously watched the same relevant opening titles, sequences which gradually became engrained in our memory. One such sequence served as the memorable opening for an action adventure series starring Lee Majors.

For those of you old enough to remember *The Six Million Dollar Man* when it first aired, if someone were to casually mention the series to you now, you would likely do one of two things.

1. Belt out the famous theme tune, while pretending to run in slow motion on the spot. "Da, da, da, daaa..."
2. Adopt your best serious look, while dramatically intoning, "Gentleman, we can rebuild him. We have the technology."

In just under ninety seconds, the opening titles to *The Six Million Dollar Man* gave us succinct details of the events which led to former astronaut Colonel Steve Austin undergoing experimental surgery to make him the world's first bionic human. That short sequence, playing almost like a film trailer, did a fine job of whetting our appetites for what was to come. Viewing the opening again while writing this book gave me goosebumps, happy memories of watching *The Six Million Dollar Man* with my parents still

A Six Million Dollar Man lunch box, just a small part of the 70s merchandise craze. (Image: Keith Homan/Shutterstock)

seeming fresh in my mind. As mentioned earlier in the book, I, along with millions of other kids around the world, also spent many happy hours playing with the *Six Million Dollar Man* action figure, one of the most fondly remembered childhood toys of its, or indeed any other, generation.

After a clutch of pilot TV movies in 1973, *The Six Million Dollar Man* series first aired in 1974 and would run for five seasons through to 1978. Of the ninety-nine episodes, undoubtedly the most famous is the one where Steve Austin comes across the legendary Bigfoot.

One of the most enduring of urban legends, supposed real-life sightings of Bigfoot (or Sasquatch as it is also known) have been claimed for years but seemed to reach a peak during the seventies. The inclusion of a Bigfoot character in *The Six Million Dollar Man* tapped into the surge of interest amongst the American public at the time for this mythical creature.

Inevitably, the bionic hero Austin, surrounded by dense forest, would engage in a huge fight with Bigfoot. It was like someone had asked one of those hypothetical 'who would win in a fight between' questions and Austin and Bigfoot had endeavoured to provide an answer. It was a fight for the ages, with Bigfoot pulling a large tree out of the ground at one point and using it to clobber Austin to the floor.

The behemoth Bigfoot was portrayed by the appropriately huge real-life wrestler Andre the Giant, the mass of fur in which he was covered making the iconic grappling star appear to be even bigger than his actual seven-foot frame.

With the character of Steve Austin becoming such an iconic hero around the world, there was every danger that Lee Majors would find it difficult to escape from the role when *The Six Million Dollar Man* eventually ended in 1978. However, the likeable star managed to avoid being typecast and, in 1981, landed another memorable TV role, that of stunt man turned bounty hunter Colt Seavers in *The Fall Guy*.

While not quite as memorable as the opening titles for *The Six Million Dollar Man*, the credits for *The Dukes of Hazzard* did feature a truly memorable and instantly recognizable theme song. Written and performed by country music legend Waylon Jennings, *Good Ol' Boys* remains a fixture in my personal list of greatest TV theme tunes. It was released as a single in the USA, peaking just outside the top twenty of the Billboard chart. A member of the Country Music Hall of Fame, Jennings also served as the narrator for *The Dukes of Hazzard*, his rough-hewn, Southern twang adding an extra layer of backwater charm to the adventures of cousins Bo and Luke Duke of Hazzard County, Georgia.

Debuting in the States on 26 January 1979 and in the UK just over a month later on Saturday 3 March, *The Dukes of Hazzard* proved hugely popular on both sides of the Atlantic, ensuring the series a decent longevity. Running for seven series, it can't be denied that the vast majority of the one hundred and forty seven episodes employed virtually the same plot. The Duke boys would be falsely accused by shady county commissioner Boss Hogg of committing a crime. Aided by cousin Daisy and wily old Uncle Jessie, Bo and Luke would then set out to prove their innocence by capturing the real criminals, often out-of-town villains employed by Boss Hogg himself. A number of car chases and plentiful cries of 'yee-haw' would follow, before all was well once again in Hazzard County.

Using the same few plot devices each time actually lent the series a feeling of cosy familiarity. You always knew where you were with *The Dukes of Hazzard* and exactly what you were going to get. When that included the always welcome sight of Catherine Bach in exceedingly skimpy denim shorts, then that was perfectly alright with me. Indeed, so memorable was the image of Bach as Daisy, the brief, tight-fitting style of denim shorts she wore became known thereafter as 'daisy dukes'. Many a Saturday tea-time, my forkful of chilli con carne came to a halt just outside my gaping mouth as Daisy Duke, shorts and all, clambered gracefully out of another muscle car. What a chassis.

In addition to cousin Daisy's shorts-clad rear and Uncle Jessie's silky white beard, *The Dukes Of Hazzard* also featured one of the most iconic of all television vehicles, the Duke boys' pride and joy, the General Lee. A customised 1969 Dodge Charger, the General Lee featured a Confederate flag on the roof in keeping with the show's Southern setting. The Duke boys unfortunately suffered from a rare allergy to car door handles, necessitating energetic leaps through the window when entering the car. Perhaps to alleviate the tension brought on by the allergy, the cousins would also regularly slide across the General Lee's orange bonnet too.

I have nothing but fond memories of *The Dukes of Hazzard*. Saturday tea-times on BBC1 were never quite the same after Bo, Luke and the General Lee disappeared down that dirt track for the final time.

During the eighties, Saturday tea-time telly was a veritable goldmine for lovers of action adventure series from the US. With *The Dukes of Hazzard* reigning supreme on BBC1, ITV needed a smash-hit import of their own in order to compete. They found it with *The A-Team,* a show which actually shared some common ground with its BBC rival. Both series were very formulaic, featuring plots which varied very little from episode to episode. Also each show could boast an iconic motor vehicle.

While the Duke cousins had the General Lee, B.A. and the boys rode around in a customised GMC van. Jet black with a distinctive red stripe running across the sides and just over the front grille, this was a highly distinctive, cool looking vehicle. In storyline terms though, this GMC was a little too distinctive. As fugitives on the run from the military, these boys didn't seem too concerned with being spotted did they? Then again, *The A-Team* was never a series that could be accused of being steeped in reality.

The pilot episode of *The A-Team* first aired on the NBC network in the United States on Sunday 23 January 1983. When the first regular episode was broadcast the following Sunday immediately after the Super Bowl, it garnered huge ratings and gave the series a head start in terms of building a fan base. We only had to wait six months before ITV began to broadcast *The A-Team* in the UK, the first episode airing on a Friday evening in July. The series moved to its familiar Saturday tea-time slot with the airing of the second season.

If you had never seen an episode of *The A-Team* and had simply read a synopsis of the series, you could be forgiven for believing it to be a gratuitously violent, masochistic exercise suitable only for an adult audience. The sheer amount of gunplay featured in each episode was normally off the scale. However, as we all know, nobody was ever killed by gunfire or, it seemed, badly wounded. Not only could the bad guys withstand heavy artillery fire clad only in faded dungarees and a red neckerchief, they also possessed the ability to walk away unscathed from multiple vehicle crashes. It was an unwritten rule that every episode of *The A-Team* had to feature slow-motion footage of a pick-up truck rolling over in mid-air, before coming to an unceremonious halt on dusty ground, roof-side down. The fact that nobody was ever seriously hurt by gunfire may not have been the best message to children watching the show but each episode always ended with the bad guys paying for their crimes, which was a positive in terms of teaching youngsters that crime really does not pay. Mind you, I was never into all that message malarkey when I was a

Superb publicity shot of the one and only Mr T in The A Team. (Photo: MCA TV)

kid. I simply watched *The A-Team* because it was fun and I wanted to see Mr. T kick some ass.

Speaking of the man born Laurence Tureaud, when *The A-Team* movie reboot was released in 2010, the eighties icon was quick to put on record his dislike of the numerous violent deaths featured in the updated version.

"When we did it nobody got hurt and it was all played for fun and entertainment. These seem to be elements nobody is interested in anymore."

Although the characters of Colonel 'Hannibal' Smith (George Peppard), Face (Dirk Benedict) and 'Howling Mad' Murdock (Dwight Schultz) were all popular in their own right, it was B.A. Baracus, the bad tempered tough guy with the heart of gold, who captured the public's attention, turning Mr T into a global phenomenon. During the eighties, there weren't many people who did not know who Mr T was. Mind you, with his muscled frame, Mohawk hairstyle and body adorned with a heavyweight mass of jewellery, he was never going to go unrecognised.

Spin-off merchandise featuring the distinctive action star was everywhere in the eighties. In addition to the inevitable official *A-Team* products, companies were keen to turn Mr T himself into a brand. From stationary sets and air fresheners to action figures and comics, the likeable star's face was everywhere. There was even a Mr T Cereal with each of the pieces in the shape of the letter T.

While Laurence 'Mr T' Tureaud was one of the faces of the eighties, for me *The A-Team* was the series that truly defined the decade's television from across the pond. From 1983 to 1987, if we had a problem and no one else could help, we always knew we could hire *The A-Team*. That's if we could find them of course.

During the writing of this book, the CBS television network in the states announced a remake of *Magnum P.I.* their hit action series from the eighties. While I always prefer to reserve judgment on reboots such as this until I have actually seen the finished product, I have to admit to having serious doubts in this case. Although original star Tom Selleck, now aged 73, is too advanced in years to race around the Hawaiian islands in a Ferrari while wearing shorts and a hideously loud shirt, there is no escaping the fact that Tom Selleck IS Magnum and Magnum IS Tom Selleck.

An iconic image from the original *Magnum* which will be sadly missing from the remake is Selleck's moustache. Almost as famous as the man himself, Tom's upper lip hair will likely go down in history as the greatest telly 'tache of them all, beating worthy contenders such as the one worn by Peter Wyngarde as playboy detective *Jason King* and that of *Grandstand* legend Des Lynam. *Only Fools and Horses* star John Challis, who still sports an iconic moustache of his own, once told me that Tom Selleck's moustache was 'soft and luxuriant'. This was from first-hand experience too, he and his wife having once spent time relaxing on a beach in Hawaii with Selleck himself. Incidentally, Jay Hernandez, the actor chosen to play the new Magnum, will do so clean-shaven. For shame.

It will be difficult to capture the spirit of the original as *Magnum P.I.* was a product of its time. The glitz and glamour that defined eighties telly was much in evidence in *Magnum*, due in no small part to the fabulous red Ferrari 308GTS driven by the private detective and also the exotic location in which the series was set. To ensure that the character of Magnum was in some way relatable to the viewers at home, it was pointed out early on in the show's run that the snazzy Ferrari was not actually his. Instead, it belonged to Magnum's employer, the reclusive and extremely wealthy writer Robin Masters, who allowed the private investigator to live on his huge estate in exchange for his services as a security consultant.

Behind the scenes shot of Tom Selleck filming Magnum PI in 1984. (Photo: Alan Light)

In light of his reclusive nature, the character of Masters was never seen, although we did hear his voice on a few occasions (a voice provided by Orson Welles no less).

Also living on the Masters estate was the prim and proper former Sergeant Major from the British Army, Jonathan Higgins. As the keeper of the house, it was Higgin's job to ensure the smooth running of the estate in the absence of Robin Masters, a job role that often brought him into comical conflict with the laid-back Magnum.

For me, that special interplay between Magnum and Higgins was the very heart of the show. As the series progressed, the relationship between the two polar opposites was explored further when it became obvious to producers that this interplay was the highlight for many viewers.

John Hillerman was simply marvellous as the pompous but loveable Higgins, his on-screen chemistry with Tom Selleck helping to propel *Magnum P.I.* to classic television status. Both actors fittingly won awards for their performances, each winning a Golden Globe and an Emmy. Hillerman was the first to be officially recognised, collecting the Golden Globe for Best Supporting Actor in 1982. This was complemented with a supporting actor Emmy in 1987. Tom Selleck received his Emmy for Outstanding Lead Actor in a Drama Series in 1984 and the equivalent Golden Globe in 1985.

Employing an impeccable English accent as the upper-crust estate manager, it comes as something of a surprise to learn that John Hillerman was actually born in the city of Denison in Texas. Earlier in his career, he had played English characters a number of time on stage, so by the time the role of Higgins came to him, he was well-versed in the vocal patterns of those born in England.

Higgins' oft-repeated utterance of the phrase "Oh my God", usually when in a state of exasperation due to the actions of Magnum, was a favourite in the school playground as my friends and I recounted the happenings of the latest episode from the evening before.

These school discussions usually took place on a Monday morning as *Magnum* was regularly broadcast on a Sunday afternoon, a time slot fondly recalled by many of us, including comedian Peter Kay who, during one of his stand-up routines included *Magnum* in the list of series he and his family would watch on a Sunday, usually after *Bullseye* had finished. Whenever I hear that upbeat, exciting *Magnum* theme tune, memories of my own lazy Sunday afternoons spent watching telly and munching biscuits come flooding back.

Although set in a similarly exotic location, transferring the action from Hawaii to Miami, the trend-setting *Miami Vice* was far grittier than *Magnum P.I.* It also had a look that was most assuredly all its own. If you are looking for a TV series to perfectly sum up the fashion and cultural landscape of the USA during the eighties decade, then look no further than *Miami Vice*.

As a teenager at the time that *Miami Vice* was first broadcast in the UK, the fashions featured in the series had a big influence on me, as I am sure they did with many others my age.

Teenage boys wanted to dress like Don Johnson, while teenage girls just wished that we looked like Don Johnson, even just a slight resemblance would have sufficed. As far as I can recall, no British teenage male was ever mistaken for Mr Johnson during the eighties. We really didn't stand a chance. After all, while his outfits screamed expensive designer labels, ours simply muttered Man at C&A. Nonetheless, I wore my grey flecked jacket with pride, the cuffs rolled a short distance up the arm, as per the unwritten law of eighties male fashion. I also recall owning a white cotton jacket with puffed sleeves and an integrated belt that served no purpose other than to hang jauntily down at the front. While Don Johnson's on-screen alter ago Sonny Crockett donned his fashionable threads to cruise the streets of South Beach, Miami in a Ferrari Testarossa, I sported my white cotton jacket in a forlorn bid to appear cool while sitting on the top deck of the 535 bus to Wolverhampton.

In addition to the distinctive look of the show, the creative minds behind *Miami Vice* also made a concerted effort to make the series sound different too. In what could almost be described as a bid to capture the imagination of the MTV generation, the soundtrack of each episode would usually feature at least one recognisable contemporary hit record, the featured artists including the likes of Depeche Mode, Billy Idol, Frankie Goes to Hollywood, Bryan Adams, Pink Floyd and Kate Bush. At the time, the use of original hit recordings to set the mood for a scene and therefore enhance our emotional attachment to what we were watching was radical for a prime-time television cop show.

The greatest example of this technique occurred during the pilot episode of *Miami Vice*. As Crockett and Tubbs drive through the darkened streets of Miami in Crockett's black Ferrari Daytona Spyder, on their way to a showdown with drugs kingpin Calderone who had been responsible for the death of Tubbs' brother, the sombre drumbeats of *In the Air Tonight* by Phil Collins permeate the air. The increasing tension in Collins' musical masterpiece matches the escalating on-screen drama to perfection as the two cops stare stoically into the darkness, exchanging only the odd word, each knowing that they may not survive the night. At one point, Crockett stops off at a phone booth to call his ex-wife, asking her if what they once had was 'real' before trailing off into silence. Due to the almost unbearable rising tension and dark air of foreboding, this scene has remained with me to this very day. It is television at its absolute finest.

Towards the end of its near six year run, *Miami Vice* began to look tired. The overall feel of the show now seemed too dark, exuding a bleakly sombre tone which even the pounding beat of Jan Hammer's famous theme tune could not lighten.

When the final episode of *Miami Vice* aired, it signalled the end of a golden age for US TV cop shows.

The new breed of crime dramas which would populate the telly schedules during the nineties, such as *L.A. Law* and *NYPD Blue,* just didn't appeal to me in the same way that *Starsky and Hutch* had in the seventies, despite being of undoubted quality. Many of the American cop series from the seventies and eighties had an element of humour running through them, making them exceedingly entertaining to watch. Even the grittiest moments in a series such as *Miami Vice* would not have landed such a powerful dramatic blow had there not been a touch of light relief elsewhere in the episode to balance things out.

Cops and private detectives seemed to be all over the box when I was younger. How often I would get to watch a particular show was often dependent on the time of broadcast. Late nights during the week, usually after the watershed, were normally off limits due to the supposed delight of attending school the next morning. Luckily, the good old BBC, the UK home for many of the greatest imported cop shows of the time, would often broadcast my favourite series on a Saturday evening when I could stay up a lot later. Failing that, if they were scheduled for a night in the week, it would be at the more acceptable time of around 8pm. Thank you BBC.

Starsky and Hutch was part of a stellar Saturday night line-up on BBC1 in the mid-seventies, often sandwiched between *The Two Ronnies* and *Match of the Day*, with *Parkinson* rounding things off at the end of the evening. *Starsky and Hutch* is arguably the most famous of all the cop shows from this particular era, with most people of a certain age retaining fond memories of Saturday nights spent in front of the box, their senses dazzled by a bright red Ford Gran Torino and Dave Starsky's collection of chunky cardigans. All of the key ingredients necessary for a successful seventies TV cop show were present and correct; a distinctive car, cops with quirks (Starsky loved his car and his knitwear, while Hutch was a sensitive ladies man), an action-packed opening credits sequence accompanied by a rousing theme tune, a memorable supporting character (Huggy Bear) and regular car chases along the back-streets and alleyways of the city.

Most people had their favourite when it came to the two heroic title characters. Some preferred the more sensitive, occasionally slightly reserved, nature of David Soul's Ken Hutchinson, while others were attracted to the brooding qualities of David Starsky, played by Paul Michael Glaser. I was one of the few exceptions to the rule, as I didn't really have a favourite, although, in the fashion stakes, I must admit I much preferred the stylish look of Hutch's brown leather jacket to the heavyweight cardigan collection of Starsky. How he managed to avoid heatstroke wearing those monstrosities in the middle of the Californian summer I will never know.

Both David Soul and Paul Michael Glaser went on to enjoy further career success after *Starsky and Hutch* ended in 1979, although neither man has ever really fully shaken off the link with the two iconic cops. Glaser, having already directed a handful of *Starsky and Hutch* episodes, went on to further acclaim as a director, taking the helm of films such as *The Running Man* with Arnold Schwarzenegger.

At the height of his fame as Hutch, David Soul mounted a successful assault on the pop charts. *Don't Give Up on Us* and *Silver Lady,* two fairly saccharine but incredibly catchy ballads, both hit the number one spot in the UK charts in 1977. Although his on-screen acting career slowed a little after the success of *Starsky and Hutch,* Soul has found much success on the stage, particularly in musicals. In 2004, he took on the lead role in *Jerry Springer: The Opera* at the Cambridge Theatre in London's West End, a performance which was filmed by the BBC for broadcast in 2005.

For many people, myself included, there is one other television production starring David Soul which rivals *Starsky and Hutch* in terms of nostalgic memories. That production is *Salem's Lot*.

Based on the brilliant and terrifying 1975 novel by horror maestro Stephen King, *Salem's Lot* was one of the most talked about television events of 1979 in the US. We had to wait until September 1981 before we could experience the same thrill ride here in the UK, BBC1 broadcasting the first of the two epic two-hour episodes on a Monday evening at 9:25pm.

After waiting a full two years since the original American transmission, the anticipation for *Salem's Lot* on British television reached fever pitch. Although we were only eleven at the time, myself and many of my friends at school had been allowed to stay up and watch *Salem's Lot*, even though it was shown on a school night. Although video recorders were starting to become more widespread as the eighties began, many homes were still without one in 1981 due to the astronomical price of the machines at the time. Hence, it was necessary for many of us to stay up and watch the terrifying events of *Salem's Lot* unfold as they were broadcast.

I can remember the excited chatter in the playground the morning after each episode was broadcast, particularly when we first got to see the main vampire Mr Barlow. In King's original novel, Barlow was a handsome, debonair businessman. However, the television adaptation went for the shock factor with Barlow presented as a mute, hairless supernatural creature in the mould of Nosferatu. When the terrifying, exceedingly vicious vampire made his first appearance, yellow eyes blazing, rat-like teeth bared and dripping saliva, every viewer in the country jolted out of their seat. It was the type of shared viewing experience that has sadly been consigned to the past. With such a huge variety of channels to choose from today, in addition to a surfeit of online viewing options, it is highly unlikely that a large percentage of the viewing audience will all be watching the same programme. Even then, there is every chance we won't all be at the same point of the show, thanks to live pause and +1 channels.

The original *Salem's Lot* novel remains my favourite Stephen King book and I believe the 1979 television mini-series of the same name to be the greatest of all the screen adaptations of his work. It will certainly linger long in my memory.

The term 'mini-series' was first coined in the mid-seventies when the American network ABC adapted the Irwin Shaw novel *Rich Man, Poor Man* into a twelve part serial in 1976. Although not strictly the first mini-series, *Rich Man, Poor Man* was such a huge success it is generally considered the forerunner for the genre. I was too young at the time of broadcast to really remember *Rich Man, Poor Man* but I do have memories of watching a few snippets of arguably the most famous mini-series of all-time, *Roots*, just a couple of years later. Attracting unprecedented audience figures in the USA, *Roots* was one of the biggest television events of the decade.

My personal favourite mini-series, which I watched religiously when it was first broadcast, is *Shogun*. The original novel by James Clavell upon which *Shogun* was based was a truly epic tome, weighing in at over

1100 hundred pages. I remember buying the book after enjoying the television adaptation so much. However, no matter how hard I tried, I couldn't get all the way through it as it was just too long.

Adapting such a huge, swirling historical novel as *Shogun* was certainly a challenge but the NBC network pulled it off with aplomb. Running for nearly ten hours, *Shogun* was broadcast over five consecutive nights in 1980 and proved to be a runaway hit with viewers.

Filmed entirely on location in Japan, *Shogun* told the story of seventeenth-century English ship pilot John Blackthorne, who, along with his crew, finds himself shipwrecked in feudal Japan after a storm forces his ship ashore. At odds with both the Japanese culture and the Portuguese traders and Jesuit priests who reside there, Blackthorne also finds himself thrust into the middle of a bitter war between samurai warlords Toranaga and Ishido, who are battling to claim the title of Shogun, military commander of Japan.

With stunning locations and the Japanese characters speaking in their native language with no English subtitles provided, *Shogun* really did feel authentic. It was easier for viewers to empathise with the character of Blackthorne, stranded in a foreign land and facing a formidable communication barrier, when we were unable to understand the words being spoken ourselves.

Richard Chamberlain was simply superb as Blackthorne, balancing a romantic, often heroic side with displays of mistrust and occasional flashes of ruthlessness. Already a heartthrob from his days as the squeaky-clean Dr Kildare in the sixties, Chamberlain wooed female audiences all over again as the bearded, swashbuckling John Blackthorne. No doubt the female audience appreciation of Mr Chamberlain led to his casting in the later mini-series *The Thorn Birds*, which seemed to be on viewing list of every mom in the land in 1983.

A word of appreciation must also go to the late Japanese acting legend Toshiro Mifune who was a tower of magnificence in the role of the mighty Lord Toranaga. Speaking of legends, the narration which opened and closed each episode was provided by none other than Orson Welles, adding a further touch of class to proceedings.

After not seeing it for many years I recently watched *Shogun* again in its entirety. Often, after a period of absence, television series which you once loved can feel like a let-down when viewed once more. This was certainly not the case with *Shogun*. As soon as that dramatic theme music began and the familiar faces of the actors appeared in the credits sequence I was hooked. Drama, action, romance, political intrigue, feuding samurai warlords, stunning Japanese locations, what more could a person want from a mini-series?

Just before we move on from this most wonderful of mini-series, one of my all-time favourite pieces of telly trivia involves *Shogun*. So, if you are ever looking for a conversation starter, ask your friends the following question 'What was the very first American television network program in which a character uttered the word 'piss'?' Impress your mates still further by informing them that it was Richard Chamberlain himself who spoke the hallowed word, his character Blackthorne exclaiming in the very first *Shogu*n episode, "I piss on you and your country."

While a mini-series is defined as having a set amount of episodes over a defined period of time, an ongoing serial has no agreed limit on either episode numbers or length of time. Undoubtedly, my favourite ongoing serial and indeed one of my all-time favourite television shows period, is *Dallas*.

My wife expressed much surprise when I first told her many years ago that I had been an avid follower of the trials and tribulations of the oil-rich Ewing family during the eighties. She thought I would have found it all a bit too 'trashy'. While *Dallas* did veer more towards the sillier side of things during its final seasons, I always found it a cut above its main rival for the soap crown, *Dynasty*. To me, *Dynasty* was simply a pale imitation, a vastly inferior show which I actually did think of as being a 'bit trashy'. There's nothing wrong with being trashy of course. It certainly never did Dusty Bin any harm. I just thought that the Carrington family were a step below the Ewings.

Despite the magnificent Joan Collins pulling out all the stops as the deliciously bitchy Alexis, there was only room for one person at the very top of the US soap villain tree and that spot was permanently reserved for J.R. Ewing.

Played with such gleeful relish by the late and much-missed Larry Hagman, the ruthless Texas oil baron J.R. Ewing must surely go down in history as one of the greatest television characters of them all. Obsessed with money and power, J.R. tricked and schemed his way through both his professional and business lives. The eldest son of Jock Ewing, J.R. was not above cheating his own family in order to gain sole control of the family business, Ewing Oil. A serial womaniser, he regularly cheated on his long-suffering wife Sue Ellen with a string of mistresses. In one of his most heinous acts, the despicable rogue happily

The great Larry Hagman, one of my all-time television heroes. (Photo: Tinseltown/Shutterstock)

signed the papers which committed Sue Ellen to a sanitarium.

Despite all of this, viewers across the world just could not get enough of bad old J.R. He truly was the man we loved to hate. As such, both the character and the man who played him, became essential to the continued success of the show. However, the character of J.R. was not originally intended to be the lynchpin of the series.

When *Dallas* began in 1978, the emphasis was very much on the younger Ewing brother Bobby, played by former *Man from Atlantis* Patrick Duffy, and his new bride Pamela, portrayed by a very easy on the eye Victoria Principal. Their blissful union was not welcomed by all, as Pam was a member of the Barnes clan, the sworn enemies of the Ewings. It was this potentially explosive situation which drove the storylines in the early episodes. This first season of Dallas only consisted of five episodes, the first of which was broadcast on CBS on 2 April 1978. UK viewers were able to pay their first visit to Southfork on Tuesday 5 September 1978. Such was the success of these opening episodes, CBS commissioned a lengthier second series.

It wasn't long before the focus shifted from the relationship of Bobby and Pam to the devious dealings of elder Ewing brother J.R. By the time the third series aired, *Dallas* was fully into its stride and Larry Hagman was the undisputed star of the show. Already one of the highest rated shows on television as the new decade dawned, *Dallas* was about to go into overdrive and a new merchandising craze born.

On 21 March 1980, the final episode of the third series of *Dallas* was broadcast in the United States. The climax of the show saw a mystery assailant shoot J.R. in his Ewing Oil office as he worked late at night.

As the ruthless businessman slumped to the floor, presumed dead, the final credits rolled. It was the birth of the cliffhanger. With J.R. having been particularly heinous during the preceding episodes of series three, there was certainly no shortage of suspects. Among his many dirty deeds, he had driven his wife Sue Ellen back to the bottle, left the professional career of his bitter rival Cliff Barnes in ruins, begun a torrid affair with Sue Ellen's younger sister Kristin and, through his underhand business dealings, led Bobby and Pam to make the decision to move out of Southfork.

The riddle of who shot the man we all loved to hate became one of the biggest television phenomenons of all-time. The slogan 'Who Shot J.R?' could be seen on t-shirts, mugs and coasters everywhere you went. Not a day went by without some kind of mention in the press. It was even featured on the BBC News. Although I had only just turned ten at the time, I can remember the craze vividly.

Bookmakers had been laying odds on the guilty party with Sue Ellen's lover Dusty Farlow, presumed dead in a plane crash, the favourite. Other suspects included Sue Ellen herself, Cliff Barnes, Bobby and even dear old Miss Ellie.

It was a long seven months before the identity of the would-be assassin was revealed in the episode 'Who Done It?', the fourth instalment of series four. Broadcast in the UK on Saturday 21 November 1980, just a day after the US screening, millions of viewers were finally put out of their misery when it was revealed that Kristin Shepard was the person with her finger on the trigger.

Approximately 83 million people tuned in to this historic episode in the United States, the programme claiming an amazing 76% audience share that night.

The worldwide audience figure was estimated to be an astonishing 350 million. Incredible.

Dallas would feature many more end of season cliffhangers throughout the rest of the eighties, including the infamous resurrection of Bobby Ewing in Pam's shower, but it would prove an impossible task to top the frenzy which surrounded 'Who Shot J.R?'

Patrick Duffy, Linda Gray and Larry Hagman, the three mainstays of Dallas, at the Screen Actors Guild Awards in 2012. (Photo: s_buckley/Shutterstock)

BRACE YOURSELF RODNEY – PROPER COMEDY

I could happily sit and write about comedy forever, particularly that of the British variety. It is the genre which has had the most influence on me throughout my life and the one which sparked my writing career. Apart from one, all of my previous books have been comedy-related. The vast majority of my personal television heroes are associated with the comedy genre – Ronnie Barker, Sid James, David Jason, Ronnie Corbett and Rowan Atkinson to name just a few.

In my opinion there are not enough comedy programmes on television today, certainly not in Britain anyway. There seems to be an unhealthy obsession with producing cheap, tacky reality TV in which desperate, fame-hungry air-heads choose to live their lives in full view, yet still slather themselves in fake tan in order to cover any imperfections.

While reality junk takes up a criminally large proportion of the schedules, serious drama fills the majority of the remaining programme slots. There is no doubting the outstanding quality of much of today's drama output, nor its popularity. On a personal level however, I find it all just too depressing. A bit of light relief is needed. Television should be all about escaping from the sometimes harsh realities of life. We need to laugh and smile. It is good for us both physically and mentally.

As with children's television, the comedy genre experienced its golden age during the seventies and throughout the majority of the eighties. Once again, I count myself so fortunate to have been born in 1970, as it meant I was there when undisputed classics of the genre such as *Fawlty Towers* and *Porridge* were first broadcast. I may have been a bit too young to appreciate them fully at the time, that would come a little later during repeat showings, but at least I can say I was there when Basil Fawlty goose-stepped his way into small-screen immortality or when Ronnie Barker first popped into Ronnie Corbett's hardware shop to pick up four candles (or was it fork handles?)

Speaking of Messrs. Barker and Corbett, *The Two Ronnies* was a particular favourite of mine during my childhood and early teenage years. Along with their contemporaries Morecambe and Wise, Ronnie B and Ronnie C ruled the light-entertainment world during the seventies and early eighties. Their continued presence on our screens on a Saturday night was somehow comforting. All was right with the world when *The Two Ronnies* beamed into our living rooms. Along with the hugely likeable personalities of the two stars, the rigid format of *The Two Ronnies*, something which hardly changed throughout the sixteen-year run of the show, helped to create that feeling of comforting familiarity.

Each show would begin with Mr B and Mr C reading us a few items of news from behind a desk, before the first sketch aired, which was nearly always set at a party. Then we would be treated to one of Ronnie Barker's brilliant monologues. Usually portraying a spokesman for a ridiculous organisation, such as the Loyal Society for the Relief of Sufferers from Pispronunciation, Barker's deft, deadpan delivery of devilishly intricate wordplay, written by the man himself, was always a joy to behold.

My younger self always got a bit restless during the special guest singer slot. The music of Elaine Paige and Barbara Dickson didn't really appeal to many young boys like myself. I was more of a 'Motorhead on Tiswas' kind of kid.

Another sketch would usually follow before the next instalment of one of the duo's famous serials. Brilliant pastiches of old-style adventure serials in which every episode ended on a cliffhanger, the likes of The *Phantom Raspberry Blower of Old London Town* and *The Worm That Turned* have attained iconic status in their own right.

Ronnie Corbett's solo spot, delivered from his famous chair, would often come next in the running order. The diminutive comedian would tell the audience a joke, veering off on all manner of tangents before finally reaching the punchline. The fact that Corbett made it look like he was ad-libbing most of these routines, when actually they were all carefully scripted, is a testament to his supreme skill as a live performer.

The finale to each show would be a big musical number, with Barker and Corbett merrily singing along to familiar classical or big band pieces, comedy lyrics usually written by Barker. A few late items of news would follow, before the utterance of the now legendary "It's goodnight from me...and it's goodnight from him".

Despite the use of double-entendres, sometimes quite risqué once you were old enough to understand them, *The Two Ronnies* was most definitely a family show. There was never anything included which could be considered properly offensive. It was perfect Saturday night viewing for both young and old. As a perfect example of this wide-ranging appeal, many of my fondest memories of *The Two Ronnies* are of the

The Two Ronnies featured on the brilliant Royal Mail Comedy Greats Collection in 2015. (Image: Royal Mail)

times I watched the show while at my nan's house, particularly the Christmas specials. *The Two Ronnies* was always a huge deal at Christmas in our house and indeed at my nan's. In fact, even though Morecambe and Wise were the standard bearers for festive television fayre, I always looked forward more to *The Two Ronnies*. At the time, we would often spend the early-evening portion of Christmas Day at my nan's house. It never took us too long to get there as, quite conveniently she lived in the same street as us.

I remember that for many years my nan had one of those silver tinsel-type Christmas trees that were all the rage in the seventies and eighties. You would always see them pop up in the window of Woolworths as the festive season approached. The next time you watch a Christmas special of a sitcom from the *Proper Telly* era, check out the tree. I bet it's a silver one. A couple of festive editions of *The Two Ronnies* featured a silver tree looming large behind Mr Barker and Mr Corbett as they sit at their famous desk. Whenever I watch those particular shows now, I become very nostalgic for those Christmas nights spent with my nan, the Woolworth's silver special shining in the corner and everyone laughing at *The Two Ronnies* while munching on finger rolls, pork pie with egg in the middle and a Bird's Eye trifle. How did we manage to eat all of that just a few hours after devouring a huge Christmas dinner? Even if we did devour it all, the next task was trying to stay awake to enjoy the remainder of Christmas Night. The television would always remain on throughout the evening, even if it was just in the background while we played a few games. This was especially true in the pre-video recorder days. If you missed a programme back then, you would have to wait an eternity before it was repeated.

In addition to *The Two Ronnies*, Ronnie Barker was also the star of one of the greatest British sitcoms ever made. Written by Dick Clement and Ian La Frenais, *Porridge* is the Rolls Royce of television sitcoms. It remains a yardstick by which all other sitcoms should be measured. With beautifully penned scripts that concentrated on dialogue rather than contrived situations and superb performances from the entire cast, *Porridge* was a true television masterpiece.

As a kid, I must have mainly watched repeats of *Porridge* as I would have been a bit too young to appreciate the episodes when they were initially broadcast, particularly the first two series which went out in 1974 and 1975 respectively. I do remember being slightly unnerved by the fairly stark opening credits sequence which featured various heavy duty prison doors being banged shut and then locked with huge keys. Watching that as a kid was a little bit scary. However, a distinctly warm comfort would soon be at hand in the form of the wonderful Ronnie Barker.

When it comes to my personal comedy heroes, Mr Ronald William George Barker will forever hold a place at the top table. Seated alongside him at this very exclusive venue would be his long-time on-screen partner Ronnie Corbett, Sidney James, David Jason, Stan Laurel and Oliver Hardy. Now that is a table I would pay anything to be seated at.

Of all of those comedy legends, Ronnie Barker was the one who possessed the amazing ability to completely transform himself with each character he played. Compare the crafty and often cynical lag Fletch with the money-grabbing, eye-rolling shopkeeper Arkwright from *Open All Hours*. Two magnificent performances and two completely different creations.

So good was he as Norman Stanley Fletcher, I never see Ronnie Barker when watching *Porridge*. I only ever see Fletch. It was an absolutely immaculate performance from a true comedy giant. The rest of the cast really had something to live up to with Ronnie on top form but there is no doubting that they were up for the task. Richard Beckinsale as prison newbie Godber brought a beautifully light touch to his pleasingly natural performance, while Fulton Mackay was exquisitely precise in his signature role of namesake Senior Prison Officer Mackay, the perennial thorn in Fletch's side. Bringing a nice counterpoint to Officer Mackay's strict often harsh disciplinarian nature was Officer Barrowclough, a thoughtful man who believed in rehabilitation rather than punishment, an approach perhaps born out of an unhappy home life where he is obviously henpecked by his often mentioned but never seen wife. Veteran actor Brian Wilde played the seemingly forever worried Barrowclough to perfection.

Porridge is one of the very few sitcoms from the seventies that has not dated. Many comedies from this period have dated to some degree, whether it is in the form of the fashion styles of the day or the humour being of its time. Viewing *Porridge* today, you never really come across the fashion problem as the vast majority of the characters are adorned in prison issue uniforms anyway. In terms of humour, *Porridge* always seemed ahead of its time, thanks to the superior writing talent of Dick Clement and Ian La Frenais.

Another BBC sitcom which reigned supreme during the seventies and has not really suffered from dating to any great degree is *Dad's Army*. In a couple of ways, this warm nostalgic comedy shares certain similarities with *Porridge*. Both were penned by celebrated writing partnerships – for Dick Clement and Ian La Frenais substitute Jimmy Perry and David Croft. Additionally, each show featured characters clad in uniform, one prison and the other army issue. The World War II setting of *Dad's Army* also removes any danger of the series suffering from the dreaded seventies fashion problem. A major difference between the two shows was in the type of humour employed, Perry and Croft preferring a more traditional, gentle knockabout style of comedy.

In addition to *Dad's Army*, the Perry/Croft partnership created other long-running iconic sitcoms such as *It Ain't Half Hot Mum* and *Hi-de-Hi!* Each show was made in the same affectionate style and employed many of the same actors, bringing a feeling of warm familiarity to proceedings. This familiarity was heightened still further with the inclusion of the distinctive 'you have been watching' credits. Every comedy series written and produced by David Croft utilised this same style of end credit sequence, including those Croft wrote in partnership with Jeremy Lloyd, such as *Are You Being Served?* and *'Allo 'Allo!* While *Dad's Army* featured the same pre-filmed clips in its credit sequence, the likes of *Are You Being Served?* broke the fourth wall by having each actor conduct a small piece of comic business straight into camera, usually something linked with the episode in question. I loved the 'you have been watching' credits as it always seemed to me as if the members of the cast were taking a bow at the end of the show, just as they would at the conclusion of a stage production. Utilizing the services of a regular group of actors, including such familiar names as Paul Shane, Su Pollard, Jeffrey Holland, Kenneth Connor and Bill Pertwee, enhanced the cosy repertory feeling still further.

Of the many classic comedy series with which David Croft was involved, *Dad's Army* remains the most beloved. At the time of writing the show is celebrating its fiftieth anniversary, the very first episode having been broadcast on 31 July 1968. Over nine years and eighty episodes, the adventures of the bumbling but nevertheless brave members of the Walmington-on-Sea Home Guard captured the hearts of the nation.

Dad's Army was unashamedly gentle, evoking a warm feeling of cosy forties nostalgia while still managing to portray the stoic resolve of the British people in the face of extreme adversity. I think this is one of the reasons why the series has become something of a national treasure over the years. In addition to being very funny, the scripts were an affectionate tribute to the unsung heroes of Britain during the dark days of World War II; the brave men who volunteered their services for organisations such as the Home Guard and the ARP, the patriotic women who were the real backbone of the nation and the shopkeepers who kept the country stocked with supplies.

While many of the members of the Walmington-on-Sea Home Guard were comically inefficient and loveably bumbling, as veterans of previous conflicts they were brave to a man and would do anything to protect their town and the British way of life. Perhaps the bravest of all was the doddering but always willing Lance Corporal Jack Jones, mild-mannered butcher by day, fiercely determined octogenarian action man by night. Jones was always my favourite character when I was a kid and remains so to this day. As he was the character who provided most of the visual slapstick moments in *Dad's Army*, it is perhaps not surprising that Jones appealed to my younger self the most. His often-heard cries of "Don't panic!" and "They don't like it up 'em!", the latter usually accompanied by an upward thrust of his bayonet, became two of the show's most loved catchphrases, along with Fraser's pessimistic lament "We're doomed!" and, of course, Captain Mainwaring's withering putdown of young Private Pike in the form of "You stupid boy!"

When I watch *Dad's Army* today it is the lesser, more subtle Corporal Jones moments which I enjoy the most. The veteran campaigner continually being one step behind as the platoon is brought to attention never fails to start me chuckling, as does his confusion with the 24-hour clock system, "I shall be back here at six o'clock... hours!"

While it is the beautiful performances of Arthur Lowe and John Le Mesurier which normally gain the most plaudits, Clive Dunn as Lance Corporal Jones is often unfairly overlooked. Scatter-brained, fidgety and full of boundless energy for a pensioner, Jones is a wonderful comic creation. The performance of Dunn as the veteran soldier is made even more impressive when you consider that, in real life, he was only forty-eight years old when the series started and fifty-seven when it ended in 1977. Throughout his career, Clive Dunn was adept at playing doddering old men much older than his actual age. In *Bootsie and Snudge,* the sixties sequel to smash-hit comedy series *The Army Game,* Dunn played eighty-three year old Henry Beerbolm Johnson, despite being in his thirties at the time. In 1974, the fifty-four year old star took the lead role in ITV sitcom *My Old Man,* based on an original pilot which appeared on the BBC and featured Ronnie Barker in the Dunn role.

After *Dad's Army* ended, Dunn landed the title role in the children's comedy series *Grandad.* Running for four series between 1979 and 1984, the slapstick-style *Grandad* was written by the prolific Bob Block, whose most famous creation was undoubtedly *Rentaghost.* Both series were very similar in style, aimed as they were at children, and both featured memorable theme tunes. The opening theme to *Grandad* was a jaunty, music-hall style number sang by Clive Dunn himself, while the theme to *Rentaghost* will surely live forever in the memories of seventies kids everywhere. As with *Grandad*, the *Rentaghost* theme was performed by a member of the cast, in this case the late Michael Staniforth, who played the show's most enduring character, Timothy Claypole. The proliferation of children's comedy series during the seventies and early eighties ensured that the comic needs of young TV viewers were well catered for. While the quality of these shows, with the exception perhaps of

Rentaghost, was usually on the distinctly average side, in the main they were fun and undemanding to watch. In other words, they were perfect for kids. So, if you happen to come across an episode of *Metal Mickey*, *The Ghosts of Motley Hall* or *Pardon My Genie* today and find yourself groaning, just remember how much you loved them as a kid!

While the character of Lance Corporal Jones in *Dad's Army* was the role of a lifetime for Clive Dunn, originally he wasn't the only choice for the part. Indeed, Dunn almost lost out to a young, up and coming performer who also happened to be highly skilled at playing aged characters, an actor who was fully twenty years Dunn's junior. That man was a certain David Jason.

Just twenty-seven years old at the time, the future Sir David auditioned for the role of Jones after Clive Dunn had turned it down due to other work commitments. On the same day as his audition, Jason was ecstatic to be offered the part. Just hours later, Dunn found out the other show he was engaged to work in had been cancelled and producers decided to go with him for the part of Jones after all, believing the young David Jason to be too much of an unknown at this point.

However, as we all know, everything worked out just fine for the man destined to become arguably the most beloved British television star of all-time. Like his mentor Ronnie Barker, the happily down-to-earth David Jason is also one of my personal comedy heroes.

During his long and storied career, Sir David has given so many wonderful performances and provided us with a veritable cavalcade of memorable characters, many of which have attained iconic status.

Just looking solely at his comic roles is enough to warrant the likeable star his status as a television legend and a true national treasure. What a roll call of characters it is too; the shy, yearning Granville in the original *Open All Hours*, sweet old prisoner Blanco in *Porridge*, blunt Yorkshireman Ted Simcock in *A Bit of a Do* and the loveable but forever scheming Pop Larkin in *The Darling Buds of May*. On the drama front, there is the grumpy, irascible Detective Inspector Jack Frost in *A Touch of Frost*. Meanwhile, children's television has been well catered for too with Jason memorably providing the voices of *Danger Mouse*, *Count Duckula* and Toad in the beautifully idyllic Cosgrove Hall adaptation of *The Wind in the Willows*.

While all of the above roles are worthy of the highest praise, on the evening of 8 September 1981, the nation was introduced for the very first time to a certain South London market trader as BBC1 broadcast the opening episode of a brand new sitcom, *Only Fools and Horses*.

Without a doubt, Peckham wheeler-dealer Derek 'Del Boy' Trotter is one of television's finest creations. Beautifully written by the late, great John Sullivan and stunningly brought to life by David Jason, everybody loves Del. Us Brits have always pulled for the underdog, somebody who battles against the odds to be the best at what they do and ultimately prove the doubters wrong. Although Del may have conducted a few dodgy deals over the years in order to succeed, ultimately he was only trying to provide for younger brother Rodney, his grandad and latterly his Uncle Albert.

The legendary Sir David Jason, one of the most beloved British stars of all-time and a personal comedy hero of mine. (Photo: Featureflash Photo Agency/Shutterstock)

I have to admit I cannot recollect watching the first series of *Only Fools and Horses* when it was initially broadcast in 1981. Mind you, I shouldn't be too surprised at that perhaps, as this initial *Only Fools* series did not garner a great deal of attention at the time. Perhaps having little faith in the product, the BBC did not promote the show to any large degree beforehand and subsequently the first series attracted relatively low viewing figures. Thankfully, the show was recommissioned for a second series, something which television executives seem to be nervous about doing these days. By the time series three was broadcast in 1983, viewing figures had grown enormously and, as we all know, would continue to rise to record-setting levels.

If my memory serves me correctly, the very first episode of *Only Fools and Horses* I ever saw was the series two classic *The Yellow Peril*, first broadcast on Thursday 8 November 1982. In order to make use of a job lot of stolen paint purchased from Trigger, Del persuades the owner of a local Chinese takeaway to have his kitchen repainted and leaves Rodney and Grandad to do all of the work.

After finding out from Trigger that the paint is used for signs in railway tunnels and is therefore luminous, Del not only has to deal with the distraught takeaway owner whose kitchen is pulsing like a radioactive orb but also has to come to terms with the fact he has painted his mother's headstone with the same luminous substance. I can remember laughing along with my mom and dad as the three Trotters stared incredulously at the giant ostentatious headstone glowing fiercely in the darkness, Grandad lamenting the fact that the cemetery is 'on the main flight path to Heathrow'.

Wonderful visual moments such as this, usually punctuated with a devastatingly funny piece of dialogue for good measure, were a trademark of *Only Fools and Horses* and John Sullivan's writing in general. I can't think of any other British comedy series that can boast so many classic moments which will forever retain a place in the annals of comedy history.

Series two of *Only Fools and Horses*, from which came the caper with the luminous paint, also contained the episode *A Touch of Glass*, in which Del, Rodney and Grandad have a little spot of bother with a priceless chandelier. One of the greatest scenes in sitcom history, I still laugh uproariously every time I see the chandelier come crashing to the floor, right behind a disbelieving Del and Rodney. Even after all these years, when you know exactly what is going to happen, the magic of the moment has not worn thin in any way. From Grandad's low-key warning from upstairs of "One more turn, Del!" and Del's decidedly nervous utterance of "Now brace yourself, Rodney!", the unbearable tension of the moment is heightened further by the creaking of the chandelier bolt as Grandad slowly loosens it. One final smack of the bolt with a hammer and a second chandelier, situated down the hall from the one under which Del and Rodders are waiting expectantly with a tarpaulin, plummets to the floor.

The twenty-two years over which *Only Fools and Horses* broadcast to a grateful nation are littered with memorable moments such as this. Who could ever forget two life-size inflatable dolls popping up from behind the bar in the Trotter's flat after self-inflating, or Del and Rodney emerging from the mist of a dark back alley dressed as Batman and Robin? How about Del hang gliding high above the Hampshire countryside or Tony Angelino, the Singing Dustman who had trouble pronouncing his R's, belting out the Roy Orbison classic *Cwying*.

Arguably the most magical moment for most fans of *Only Fools and Horses* occurred on Sunday 8 January 1989 during the broadcast of *Yuppy Love*, the opening episode of series six. Del and Trigger, finding themselves in a trendy wine bar, are trying to impress the female clientele. Advising Trigger to play it nice and cool, Del leans nonchalantly against the bar, a bar which is no longer there as the serving hatch has just been opened. Del's perfectly straight form falls sideways straight through the opening and out of sight, before the shocked wheeler-dealer emerges decidedly the worse for wear, informing a bemused Trigger to drink up as he is cramping his style.

As the studio audience laughed uncontrollably at David Jason's superbly executed pratfall, so too we viewers at home roared gleefully along with them. This was comic business at its absolute finest, from the writing to the performances and the magnificent acrobatics of David Jason. I can recall watching the hilarity unfold along with my mom and dad, all of us weeping with laughter. Over the next few weeks, we were treated to lots more comic gold involving blow-up dolls, gold chains, séances and Rodney pretending to be fourteen-years old on a holiday to Mallorca. Such was the quality of each episode, my dad proclaimed it to be the 'greatest television series there has ever been'.

In addition to being a true comedy classic, *Only Fools and Horses* has had a major influence on my life. Indeed, it played a part in bringing my wife Lisa and I together in the first place. Before becoming involved romantically, Lisa and I were friends for a number of years. Through various conversations, we discovered we had a mutual love of British comedy, in particular *Only Fools and Horses*. We would spend many a night in the local pub happily discussing our favourite episodes and moments from the show, all the while growing closer.

After we officially became a couple, we decided to test our knowledge of *Only Fools and Horses* by asking each other quiz questions based on the show, questions which we proceeded to write down in a large notebook. The pages in the notebook began to fill rapidly as we continued our trivia quest before eventually we had a set of questions which covered every episode that had been broadcast up to that point.

That notebook remained in our magazine rack for fully fifteen years before we decided to have a go at putting the content into book form. By that point, self-publishing had overcome its initial poor reputation and was looked upon more favourably by both authors and the printing industry in general. This growth in popularity for self-publishing saw a number of major players in the publishing industry throw their weight behind it, making it easier for new authors to put their work in front of an audience.

In October 2012, *Trotter Trivia: The Only Fools and Horses Quiz Book*, co-authored by Lisa and myself, was made available for the first time. We were ecstatic, and very much surprised, at the positive reaction towards the book. Not long after publication, our regional newspaper the *Express and Star* ran a full-page feature on the book which helped enormously from a publicity point of view. We also gave complimentary copies of *Trotter Trivia* to a number of *Only Fools and Horses* cast members, including John Challis, Sue Holderness, Paul Barber, Tessa Peake-Jones and Gwyneth Strong.

Meeting many members of the cast over the years, some on multiple occasions, has been a thrill. Through us following each other on Twitter, I got to know the wonderful John Challis, who played second-hand car dealer Boycie so memorably. After first meeting John at his one-man stage show *Only Fools and Boycie*, I have been fortunate enough to meet and chat with him on numerous other occasions, each time receiving a lovely warm welcome from both he and his wife Carol.

I always find it such a thrill to meet my comedy heroes. Over the years, myself and Lisa have had the pleasure of meeting many such stars, from the casts of *Only Fools and Horses* and *Red Dwarf* to veteran comedy legends such as Leslie Phillips and Jack Douglas.

One such person which fate decreed I would never get to meet was Sid James. Sid passed away on 26 April 1976, having suffered a heart attack while on stage at the Sunderland Empire performing the massively popular farce *The Mating Season*.

I was just six years old when the tragic news of Sid's passing stunned the nation. As such, I have no real recollection of the events at the time. My main memories from 1976 revolve around the incredible summer, which had the country sweltering and, ultimately, withering under the intense gaze of a permanently blazing sun. There has never been another summer quite like it since, just as there has never been another Sid.

When comedian Rik Mayall passed away unexpectedly in 2014, there was a huge outpouring of grief from a shocked nation, which I can only equate to the levels which met Sid's death in 1976. However, while both men often played exaggerated versions of themselves, they were loved by the public for very different reasons. Rik was a force of nature much admired for his outrageous self-confidence. In complete contrast, Sid was much more like the normal man in the street. It was easy to imagine downing a couple of pints with him in the local, while enjoying a quick game of three card brag.

There was a certain warmth about Sid James. No matter whether he was playing a booze-loving, 'bird' chaser or a villainous, black-hatted cowboy, it was impossible not to like him. Maybe it was that wonderful craggy face, once memorably described as resembling a bag of knitting, which endeared him so. That infectious and marvellously dirty laugh, not unlike the sound of the last of the water disappearing down the plughole, no doubt also contributed to his innate likeability. However, perhaps the secret as to why Mr Sidney James was so loved is that he was simply 'Sid' in whatever he did.

As his career progressed, Sid the character became very much entwined with Sid the man. Indeed, it is very much a testament to Sid's supreme skills as an actor that the public found it so difficult to distinguish between the two. I, for one, cannot think of another actor, comedic or dramatic, who always looked so relaxed in front of the camera. This aura of calm, however, belied an intense professionalism and strong work ethic which never left Sid throughout his prolific career. In an era when the British film industry was perhaps at its peak, with features rolling off the production line at a phenomenal rate, 'One-Take' James was the ultimate reliable asset to have on the cast list. There was no artistic temperament here! He simply wanted to get the work done and move on to the next job.

As prolific as Sid James was in film, his body of television work is just as impressive. From *Hancock's*

Half Hour and *Citizen James* on BBC to *George and the Dragon* on commercial television, Sid starred in some of the most popular sitcoms of the day.

However, the most successful period of his TV career would begin in 1971 when the first series of the domestic sitcom *Bless This House*, produced by Thames Television, was broadcast. Running for a total of sixty-five episodes, from Tuesday 2 February 1971 right up until Sid's untimely death in 1976, *Bless This House* became one of the most popular ITV sitcoms of the seventies, regularly attracting huge viewing figures.

A stationary salesman and married father of two teenagers, the character of Sidney Abbott was a nice change of pace from the woman-chasing charmers which Sid had regularly portrayed in the Carry On films. Many of Sid's fellow *Bless This House* cast members, including Diana Coupland and Sally Geeson, have stated that the character of Sidney Abbott was perhaps the closest Sid had come to playing himself.

As with many of the comedy series produced by Thames Television at the time, *Bless This House* was undemanding to watch, an entertaining half-hour weekly slice of straightforward, simple comedy designed purely to make people laugh. Nothing pretentious, nothing ironic, nothing clever, just pure comedy. All the better for it too, I say.

Like *Porridge*, my first encounter with Bless This House would have come with one of the repeat showings. With the series coming to an unfortunate end with Sid's passing in 1976, I was too young to appreciate the show first time around. Such was the continuing popularity of *Bless This House* however, repeat showings were frequent throughout the rest of the decade and well into the eighties.

My comedy hero Sid James with Diana Coupland in a publicity photo for Bless This House. (Photo: Thames Television)

In addition to the old-fashioned style of comedy and the presence of Sid James, one of the things I have always loved about *Bless This House* is the warmth which the show radiates, a warmth which no doubt came from the real-life affection which existed between the main cast. It makes it such a happy show to watch.

When I interviewed the truly delightful Sally Geeson in 2017, she confirmed that *Bless This House* was as happy an experience to make as it was to watch. Much of this she credits to Sid James.

"He was very laid back and a very relaxed man. He set an atmosphere when we were working that made it very, very happy. It was all down to Sid, it really was."

During our chat Sally also revealed that Sid's personal favourite episode of *Bless This House* was the series six opener *The Frozen Limit*, first broadcast on Thursday 29 January 1976.

"That's when we got a freezer in. I was on the phone to my boyfriend and was giving instructions to Sid on how to open the lid. It was a very comical situation and Sid loved it."

As far as my favourite episodes go, I have always had a fondness for *If the Dog Collar Fits Wear It* which sees Sally bring home a dog called Fred whose owner is no longer able to look after it. At first reluctant to welcome Fred into the family, Sid soon becomes attached to the adorable dog, touchingly covering the pooch's ears when talking to next door neighbour Trevor about possibly having to take him to a kennel. I also like *The Day of Rest* in which Sid's plans for a quiet, relaxing Sunday are scuppered by son Mike's latest abstract sculpture and new people moving in next door.

The first episode of series five, *They Don't Write Songs Like That Anymore*, is another cracker. Determined to win a song-writing competition, Sid buys an old piano from a junk shop for £20 on which to compose his masterpiece. After poring over his song for days to no avail, Sid is finally inspired to put pen to paper after a night in the pub with Trevor.

'I love Bertha Brown, she's the biggest girl in town,
It's her bust that made the fellas all turn round.
It's a pity they're lopsided, it's the way that they're divided
One weighs nothing and the other weighs ten pound.'

As with many popular sitcoms at the time, *Bless This House* enjoyed the big-screen spin-off treatment, a film version of the much-loved series hitting cinemas in 1972. In what should come as absolutely no surprise whatsoever, due to my admiration for Sid James, the *Bless This House* film is my favourite of the many spin-offs which hit the big-screen throughout the seventies. Other television sitcoms making the transition to film during this period included *Rising Damp, Man About the House, Are You Being Served?, The Likely Lads, Steptoe and Son, George and Mildred, Nearest and Dearest, On the Buses* and *Porridge*. The quality varied enormously with *Porridge, Bless This House* and *The Likely Lads* being three of the best in my opinion, while the *Are You Being Served?* spin-off remains truly dire.

I have a great fondness for the three *On the Buses* films too and retain warm memories of watching them on television during Bank Holidays, a tradition which still persists today thanks to the great folk at ITV3. Each film in the series, *On the Buses, Mutiny on the Buses* and *Holiday on the Buses*, was made by Hammer Films, more famous of course for their classic horror output. By the beginning of the seventies, the popularity of the traditional Hammer style of horror had begun to wane and the studio was starting to struggle financially. Who would have thought the answer to their troubles would arrive in the shape of a film spin-off from a television sitcom?

The first *On the Buses* film was a stupendous box-office hit, leading to two sequels. I have to admit the humour on display in the *On the Buses* films is in no way politically correct and is as subtle as a brick to the face. However, they are all very funny and I still find them hugely enjoyable to watch, even after countless viewings over the years.

Although the style of television comedy popular in the seventies still had a place on our screens as the eighties dawned, with the likes of *The Benny Hill Show*, *Terry and June* and *Are You Being Served?* still pulling in the viewers, the comedy landscape was about to change dramatically. At 9pm on Tuesday 9 November 1982, BBC2 broadcast the very first episode of a brand new comedy series called *The Young Ones,* a title which would prove to be quite appropriate as it was ultimately loved by the young and hated by parents.

The *Radio Times* for that week described this bold new series in simple fashion – 'A new series of six comedy shows of which this is the first. Be there or be square!" *The Young Ones* itself was, of course, anything but simple. Loud, colourful and right in your face, *The Young Ones* ripped up the television comedy rule book in gloriously anarchic fashion. Fast-paced, often surreal and employing a cartoon-style of slapstick violence, *The Young Ones* was a TV tornado the like of which we had never seen before. Making huge stars of Rik Mayall, Adrian Edmondson, Nigel Planer and Alexei Sayle, names which were previously only really known to followers of the alternative comedy scene, *The Young Ones* became the definitive show of the eighties generation.

The morning after the first episode of *The Young Ones* went out on BBC2, school playgrounds up and down the country were full of excited chatter about the thirty minutes of anarchy that had been witnessed the night before. My friends and I were part of that seemingly en masse conversation, recalling our favourite bits from each show and proceeding to act them out during break times.

While at middle school we had drama lessons once a week. During these lessons we would split into small groups, usually about four pupils to a group, and be asked to create and perform sketches on a given subject. Such was the impact made by *The Young Ones* on myself and my friends, our sketches would almost always feature the characters from the show, no matter what the subject matter we had been given. I specialised in playing lentil-loving hippy Neil, while my friends portrayed violent punk Vyvyan and people's poet Rick (spelt with a silent P). We didn't bother with Mike as we thought that character to be a bit boring to be honest.

At the time, *The Young Ones* seemed liked a show that had been made just for us, a series that was not supposed to be watched by parents or other older authority figures. It was loud, it was brash, it was anarchic – three things that I most certainly was not at that age. In fact, I still do not resemble those remarks in any way now. However, I think this is why *The Young Ones* appealed to me so much at the time of initial broadcast. It provided me an opportunity to escape from reality and be anarchic in a different way, simply by watching and very much enjoying a programme that had all sorts of serious *Points of View* type grown-ups recoiling in abject disgust.

In a similar vein, the various chronicles of the *Blackadder* family, as portrayed by the sublime Rowan Atkinson, were another favourite topic of conversation at school. Although nowhere near as outrageous and childlike as *The Young Ones*, these hilarious slices of revisionist history still contained enough silly knob gags to keep your average schoolboy in permanent hysterics, particularly when Ben Elton came on board for *Blackadder II*. As with *The Young Ones*, my school mates and I would act out various scenes from the series, although as we were a little older by this point (*Blackadder II* first aired in 1985), the recreation of our favourite moments would be in the form of dialogue between ourselves rather than sketches played out in front of others. Memorable moments from *Blackadder II* which captured our attention the most include the family of jailers who were all christened with the name Ploppy, the inimitable Tom Baker chewing the scenery as the booze-soaked, flame red-bearded sailor Captain Rum and Lord Percy cracking the age-old practice of alchemy with his creation of 'green'. Let's not forget either the sight of Lord Blackadder himself placing a pair of false breasts on his head, with the pretence that they are, in fact, ear muffs. This was done in order to pacify his fiercely puritan aunt, Lady Whiteadder, who would, rather incongruously, become infatuated with a turnip that was 'exactly the same shape as a thingy'.

With each series set in a different time period and featuring a new set of characters (albeit mostly played by the same cast), it is easy to differentiate between the various *Blackadder* incarnations and, therefore, most people have a personal favourite. Although the first series, titled *The Blackadder,* had its moments, it remains perhaps the least popular of all the *Blackadder* incarnations, concentrating on looking luscious with its extensive use of real locations instead of zeroing in on the comedic aspect.

Blackadder II was markedly different to its predecessor and much improved as a result. *Young Ones* co-writer Ben Elton teamed up with *Blackadder* creator Richard Curtis to pen the scripts for this second outing, the stand-up comedian's love of convoluted dialogue and ridiculous similes shining through immediately. Due to the BBC's concern over costs, with the first series proving so expensive to produce, *Blackadder II* was studio-bound, giving the whole enterprise more of a traditional sitcom feel, albeit a period costume sitcom set in Elizabethan England.

Sporting a full beard and growing his hair out, Rowan Atkinson was the very image of a rakish Elizabethan Lord, his elegant black outfits adding the perfect finishing touch. Rather than the timid, squirming, toadying Blackadder of series one, this Edmund was a confident ladies man, a roguish charmer with a neat sideline in crafty scheming. In complete contrast, Edmund's manservant Baldrick had taken a step back evolutionary wise since the first series, his intellect in exceedingly short supply this time around.

Another of my comedy heroes, Rowan Atkinson was truly magnificent as the devilish Lord Blackadder. Indeed, I believe *Blackadder II* to be the legendary comedy star's finest hour performance wise. His impeccable delivery of each and every line is made even more remarkable when you consider that Atkinson has a rather severe stutter.

However, even the mighty Rowan Atkinson had to take a temporary back seat when a certain force of nature going by the name of Rik Mayall entered the fray. As the roaring, in-your-face Lord Flashheart, Mayall tore up the scenery, chewed it into tiny pieces and then spat it out. He simply blew everybody away and the studio audience, along with viewers at home, absolutely loved it. The fact that at one point you can clearly see Mayall's false moustache hanging off on one side doesn't detract from the scene at all. In fact, it just makes it all the funnier. Rowan Atkinson was happy to let Rik Mayall strut his stuff for the five minutes or so that Flashheart was on-screen during the opening episode of *Blackadder II*. After all, there was no way anyone could compete with Rik Mayall when it came to stealing the show.

Flashheart would, of course, return for one episode of *Blackadder Goes Forth*, this time for a lengthier stint. Just as arrogant and brash as his ancestor, Squadron Commander Lord Flashheart was the greatest British flying ace of World War I. Making another dramatic entrance, the first appearance of Flashheart drew wild applause from the studio audience and Rik Mayall preceded to steal every scene once more.

Blackadder Goes Forth boasts arguably the finest scripts of all the Blackadder series and was the perfect way for this journey through one family's history to reach its conclusion. The final scene of the very last episode, which sees our heroes go over the top into no man's land and certain death, is the most poignant, spine-tingling scene in television comedy history.

Sandwiched in between the second series and *Blackadder Goes Forth* was perhaps the most underrated of the *Blackadder* chronicles. *Blackadder the Third* saw Edmund a little lower on the social scale with no title to his name. Acting as butler to the foppish, blustering buffoon George, the Prince Regent, Edmund still possessed that famous family cunning however and was arguably the most ruthless of all the Blackadder clan. Rowan Atkinson seemed to have an extra glint in his eye as the Georgian incarnation of Edmund, perhaps a sign that he was thoroughly enjoying portraying this steelier, more ruthless version of his most famous character.

Although Rik Mayall did not appear in *Blackadder the Third*, we were still treated to a barnstorming guest appearance in the final episode by Stephen Fry as a violent, seemingly demented Duke of Wellington. Fry's physically dominant and intimidating performance was the perfect tonic for fans disappointed with the lack of Flashheart in series three.

Rowan Atkinson's fine portrayals of the various incarnations of Edmund Blackadder are among the finest in British television comedy history. They easily rank alongside Ronnie Barker's glorious performance as Fletch in *Porridge*, David Jason's seminal turn as Del Boy in *Only Fools and Horses* and John Cleese's energetic, often maniacal portrayal of Basil Fawlty in *Fawlty Towers*.

Despite the rise of alternative comedy during the eighties, there was still very much a place at the time for the more traditional form of domestic sitcom.

Light, inoffensive series such as *Fresh Fields, Don't Wait Up, Terry and June, Home to Roost* and *No Place Like Home* all proved to be exceedingly popular and thoroughly durable. This proliferation of studio-bound, traditional sitcoms simply proved that the British viewing public's desire for good, old-fashioned comedy was still strong,

Of the more traditional sitcoms broadcast during the eighties, my personal favourite was *Never the Twain*. Enjoying a healthy run of sixty-seven episodes, spread over eleven series from 1981 to 1991, *Never the Twain* had the star power of its two leads, Donald Sinden and Windsor Davies, to thank for its considerable success. Bouncing off each other to great effect, these two veterans of television comedy had a ball as rival antique dealers Simon Peel (Sinden) and Oliver Smallbridge (Davies). Former business partners, Peel and Smallbridge are now bitter rivals after a falling out. However, as next door neighbours in terms of both their homes and antique shops, the two warring dealers can't escape one another. An extra spanner is thrown into the works when Peel's son and Smallbridge's daughter get married.

Never the Twain was a comedy of one-upmanship, with each of the two main characters desperate to best the other. Simon Peel, played with a wonderful air of superiority by Donald Sinden, was an inveterate snob who regarded the likes of Smallbridge as being beneath him. The character of Oliver Smallbridge was more down to earth than Peel and proud of his working-class Welsh roots. As he was portrayed by the marvellous Windsor Davies, one of my favourite comedy actors, I always pulled for Smallbridge to come out on top in each episode. The writers were always fair though, allowing both characters the occasional victory, although the vast majority of episodes ended with neither gaining outright superiority.

Never the Twain was never going to win any awards for subtlety or innovation but frankly, who cares? It was enjoyed by millions of people and maintained its popularity for an extremely impressive ten years. The comedy was clean, simple and fun, suitable for the whole family. Best of all, the show boasted two lead actors who were at the top of their game and clearly enjoying every moment.

Never the Twain was usually broadcast on a weekday evening about 8pm. This meant I could enjoy each episode in full without having to worry about going to bed half way through as it was a school day the next day. This wasn't the case for all of the comedy series during that time however and hearing the theme tunes to certain shows today still brings back memories of dreading having to go back to school after time off.

For me, the theme which I most associate with thoughts of school the next morning is that for *Yes,*

Minister. Although the days of the week on which this most intelligent of sitcoms was broadcast varied from series to series, I still associate *Yes, Minister* with Sunday evenings. Looking back at the broadcast dates now, it was only actually the third series which went out on Sunday nights but hearing that theme tune today still takes me back to Sunday evenings at home as a kid, knowing that I would have to go to bed not long after the first notes of the *Yes, Minister* theme played. For this reason, *Yes, Minister* was never a favourite of mine when I was younger. Even without the school link, the dialogue heavy scripts and political setting didn't appeal to me anyway. That's hardly surprising really considering I was not yet even a teenager at the time. As an adult, I rank both *Yes, Minister* and its follow-up *Yes, Prime Minister* amongst the greatest British comedy series of all-time. Each script by Antony Jay and Jonathan Lynn is honed to absolute perfection and played beautifully by Paul Eddington, Nigel Hawthorne and Derek Fowlds.

For me personally, the comedy genre defines my telly-watching life more than any other. Comedy has remained my favourite form of entertainment, from my childhood days right through to the present. It has provided the basis for my writing career, given me the opportunity to meet, and in some cases befriend, actors who I truly admire and, most importantly, it brought my wife Lisa and I together in the first place. It can't get any better than that.

ALL THE RIGHT NOTES - PROPER CHRISTMAS TELLY

One of the criticisms which is often levelled at television broadcasters today is that they do not seem to want to make an effort at Christmas anymore. It is certainly true that the festive schedules are liberally peppered with depressing soap operas and (not so) special editions of programmes which can otherwise be seen throughout the year anyway.

With more channels available to viewers than ever before, not to mention the ever increasing number of ways of accessing them, it seems that quality has very much been sacrificed in order to make way for quantity. You would think that with increased competition for viewers, the networks would pull out all the stops at Christmas to gain a greater audience share. Sadly, this is not the case. The sheer amount of viewing options available today has pretty much rendered any efforts by the channels to boost ratings meaningless, as there is a greater chance of their programming simply getting lost in the giant shuffle.

Even the BBC, the last bastion of quality festive programming, seems to have lost heart over the last few years. You don't need to wait for the big Christmas edition of the *Radio Times* to come out to know exactly what the Christmas Day early evening line-up on BBC1 will be - *Strictly Come Dancing*, *Doctor Who*, *Call the Midwife*, *EastEnders* and *Mrs Brown's Boys*.

While there is nothing inherently wrong with that line-up, some would say it is just laziness on behalf of programmers to recycle the same schedule each and every year. However, this is not a new phenomenon by any means. Looking back at the Christmas Day BBC1 schedules of the seventies, it becomes apparent that a number of programmes were shown on a regular basis year on year. The major difference between then and now however is in the number of channels available. With just three to choose from before Channel Four arrived in 1982, Christmas viewing was much more of a shared experience, a traditional activity for families across the land. With no way of recording the shows and none of this +1 business, if you didn't want to miss a show you had to make sure you sat down to watch it at the time of broadcast.

Undoubtedly the biggest Christmas telly tradition of the seventies was *The Morecambe and Wise Show*. So important was it to viewers, many people would rate their entire Christmas based on their enjoyment of Eric and Ernie's latest effort. This put tremendous pressure on the legendary double-act. Eric Morecambe in particular felt the strain each year of trying to top the previous seasonal special. Throughout the decade, *The Morecambe and Wise Christmas Show* was not simply the highlight of the festive season, it was the highlight of the entire televisual year. As such, it attracted a very high calibre of guest stars.

The 1970 festive outing saw iconic horror film star Peter Cushing return to demand the money owed to him by Eric and Ern for his previous appearances on the show. Peter's regular attempts to extract the monies owed to him became one of the show's most

The legendary duo were part of the magnificent Royal Mail Comedy Greats Collection in 2015. (Image; Royal Mail)

loved running gags over the years. The legendary star even followed the duo across to ITV after they switched channels in 1977. He still never got his money.

In 1971, *The Morecambe and Wise Christmas Show* featured arguably the most famous Eric and Ern sketch of them all, as Eric Morecambe went head to head with the world-renowned conductor Andre Previn. Of course, Eric was playing all the right notes, they just weren't necessarily in the right order.

This historic moment in British comedy was not the only iconic sketch to feature in a *Morecambe and Wise Christmas Show*. In 1976, newsreader Angela Rippon stunned the nation when she emerged from behind the news desk to reveal the most wonderful pair of legs as she high-kicked her way through 'A',

You're Adorable. This very same show also saw Eric and Ernie perform their own wonderful version of Gene Kelly's *Singin' in the Rain* routine.

The 1977 *Morecambe and Wise Christmas Show* would be the last time the duo appeared on the BBC before moving to their new home of ITV the following year. They certainly went out with a bang. Attracting an incredible 21.3 million viewers, one of the largest audiences in British television history, this magical Christmas special featured a galaxy of guest stars including Arthur Lowe, John Le Mesurier and John Laurie from *Dad's Army*, Penelope Keith and Francis Matthews joining Eric and Ernie in a parody of Cyrano de Bergerac and, most memorably of all, a selection of familiar male newsreaders and presenters performing a highly energetic rendition of *There is Nothing Like a Dame* from *South Pacific*. The editing of this final piece was so impressive, you really could believe that the likes of Michael Aspel, Richard Baker, Barry Norman and Frank Bough were capable of performing somersaults and cartwheels.

Eric Morecambe and Ernie Wise will forever be associated with classic Christmas television. Amazingly though, the 1977 *Morecambe and Wise Christmas Show* was only the second highest-rated programme that day, despite attracting 21.3 million. Even more incredible is the fact that the star of the most-watched show on Christmas Day 1977, pulling in 21.4 million viewers, is now sadly forgotten by most

Along with Morecambe and Wise and The Two Ronnies, impressionist Mike Yarwood was one of the jewels in the BBC's light-entertainment crown. Throughout the seventies, *The Mike Yarwood Show* regularly attracted in excess of 18 million viewers. His impressions of the most prominent politicians of the day, including Harold Wilson and Edward Heath, are the stuff of legend. However, as a new decade dawned, Yarwood struggled to mimic the latest figures from the world of politics and entertainment, so gamely soldiered on with his stock routine. This made him look rather old-fashioned and out of date, particularly when compared with the alternative comedy scene that was sweeping the nation at the time. By 1987, Mike Yarwood had sadly faded from the limelight.

As a seventies kid, I remember there being a number of dull Christmas Day programmes scattered amongst the highlights. *Billy Smart's Christmas Circus* was an interminable seasonal telly tradition that often sapped your festive spirit. Although it was usually only on for about an hour, that sixty minutes could seem like an eternity when you were a kid. The only good thing about *Billy Smart's Christmas Circus* was that it was often broadcast just after you had eaten your Christmas dinner, meaning you could happily fall asleep and miss the entire thing. In the same category was *Holiday on Ice*. Loved by moms and nans and described in the television listings as 'the greatest live extravaganza in Europe', these deathly dull 'spectaculars' appeared with monotonous regularity every Christmas.

The Royal Mail Christmas stamps for 1970 were about as exciting as Billy Smart's Christmas Circus.

Usually sandwiched in-between *Holiday and Ice* and *Billy Smart's Christmas Circus* was a far more enjoyable seasonal tradition, the festive edition of *Top of the Pops*. Amazingly, the iconic pop programme is still very much a part of the BBC1 Christmas Day line-up today, despite the regular series coming to an end back in 2006.

The Christmas edition of *Top of the Pops* was always a big thing in our house. My brother and I would try our utmost to try and watch as much as possible from the Christmas dinner table, although usually mom would make us turn the television off. Sometimes we would be able to reach a compromise and leave the telly on but with the sound turned down to minimum.

Top of the Pops on Christmas Day would always feature the best-selling songs of the year and the show often finished with the coveted Christmas number one. Getting to the number one spot at Christmas was a major deal in those days with most record companies timing the release of new records to ensure sales reached their peak at exactly the right moment. In fact, just reaching the number one spot in the charts at all, no matter what the time of year, was a great achievement at the time. With sales of records at far greater levels than they are now, competition was fierce.

The policy of rotating the *Top of the Pops* presenters meant you could play the guessing game as to who was going to front the show on Christmas Day, as long as you hadn't already looked in the bumper edition of the *Radio Times* of course! Radio One disc jockeys you could expect to see on festive editions of *Top of the Pops* included the likes of Tony Blackburn, Noel Edmonds, Simon Bates, Kid Jensen, Mike Read, Steve Wright and Gary Davies.

While *Top of the Pops* and our dear Queen continue to feature on our screens on 25 December right to this very day, as the eighties dawned other festive telly traditions began to fall to the wayside. Morecambe and Wise lost much of their sparkle after moving from the BBC to ITV, while Mike Yarwood seemed to look more out of touch with each passing year. While *The Two Ronnies* was still as strong as ever and magician Paul Daniels raked in the viewers with his Christmas Day specials, the eighties decade would bear witness to a change in our festive viewing habits, as blockbuster Hollywood films and a certain sitcom set in Peckham, South London began to dominate the ratings.

Throughout much of the eighties and nineties, *Only Fools and Horses* was as much a part of Christmas as tinsel, turkey and those little pigs in blankets which only ever seem to be available in the shops during December. The first feature length special of *Only Fools and Horses* was the brilliant *To Hull and Back* in 1985. This was the year that the BBC and ITV went head to head on the big day, as the Beeb sent *Only Fools* into battle against ITV's *Minder*. In the battle of the cockney wide-boys, Del Boy emerged triumphant against Arthur Daley by a significant margin. By the time the classic *The Jolly Boys' Outing* was broadcast in 1989, raking in over 20 million happy viewers, *Only Fools and Horses* had become intrinsically linked with the festive season. It was the programme you circled first when perusing the big fat festive edition of the *Radio Times*, before excitedly looking at what the big film would be on Christmas Day afternoon.

The tradition of broadcasting a major film just after *The Queen's Speech* didn't really start until 1980. While many big movies had been shown on 25 December before this time, they were usually broadcast in the evening. As the eighties began, the television networks realised they could garner better ratings by switching the flagship film to the afternoon slot when many families would just be starting to settle down in front of the telly after enjoying their dinner.

For me, BBC1 was always the place to be when it came to Christmas Day films as ITV usually went with a James Bond movie, a franchise which I have never really enjoyed that much.

Here is a list of the big Christmas Day films broadcast on BBC1 for each year of the eighties. While the first few on this list may not be considered blockbusters now, at the time it was a major deal to be able to see them on the telly. Indeed, all of the films below were being shown on British television for the very first time.

    1980 - 20,000 Leagues Under the Sea (1954)
    1981 – In Search of the Castaways (1962)
    1982 - International Velvet (1978)
    1983 - Treasure Island (1950)
    1984 – Mary Poppins (1964)
    1985 – No afternoon film
    1986 – Annie (1982)
    1987 – Indiana Jones & Temple of Doom (1984)
    1988 – Back to the Future (1985)
    1989 - Crocodile Dundee (1986)

It seems rather quaint today to consider that *Mary Poppins*, one of those films that now receives an outing every holiday season, was only showing for the first time in 1984, a full twenty years after its cinema release. However, this was how things operated back then, particularly when it came to Disney films. It certainly made the broadcast of a big movie on television seem even more of a major event, something that you really did not want to miss.

That last statement could describe the whole of Christmas television in the *Proper Telly* era really. In fact, although I may well be under the influence of nostalgia here, I would happily place the majority of seventies and eighties television in categories marked 'special' and 'unmissable'.

A PROPER TELLY TRIBUTE

With this book being a personal recollection of the television landscape during the seventies and eighties, for a series to be included it has to hold particular warm memories for me. This means of course that there are certain classic programmes from the era which have unfortunately missed out, mainly because there is simply not the room to include them all.

However, it would be amiss of me to close the book without giving at least a mention to the following series which helped define the *Proper Telly* era.

All Creatures Great and Small; Angels; Animal Magic; Battlestar Gallactica; Bergerac; The Bill; The Bionic Woman; Bod; Boon; Boys from the Blackstuff; Brideshead Revisited; Buck Rogers in the 25th Century; Cagney and Lacey; Carrott's Lib; Charlie's Angels; Cheers; Cheggars Plays Pop; Columbo; Coronation Street; Crackerjack; Crossroads; Crown Court; Dave Allen at Large; The Dick Emery Show; Diff'rent Strokes; Doctor Who; EastEnders; The Equalizer; Fame; Fantasy Island; Fingerbobs; Fraggle Rock; Game for a Laugh; The Gentle Touch; George and Mildred; The Good Old Days; The Goodies; Happy Days; Hawaii Five-o; Holiday; How We Used to Live; Howard's Way; I, Claudius; The Incredible Hulk; Jamie and the Magic Torch; Juliet Bravo; Kelly Monteith; Kick Start; Kung Fu; Last of the Summer Wine; The Lenny Henry Show; Life and Loves of a She-Devil; The Life and Times of

Grizzly Adams; Little House on the Prairie; The Love Boat; Lovejoy; Man About the House; M*A*S*H; Mickey Spillane's Mike Hammer; Minder; Monty Python's Flying Circus; Nationwide; New Faces; Newsround; Only When I Laugh; The Onedin Line; Opportunity Knocks; The Paul Hogan Show; Pebble Mill at One; Play for Today; Play Away; Play School; Please Sir!; The Professionals; Record Breakers; Rising Damp; Robin of Sherwood; Robin's Nest; The Rockford Files; Roobarb; Rumpole of the Bailey; Runaround; Shine On Harvey Moon; Shoestring; Soap; Some Mother's Do 'Ave 'Em; Space 1999; Spitting Image; The Sweeney; Sykes; Take the High Road; Tales of the Unexpected; Taxi; Tenko; Terrahawks; That's Life; This is Your Life; Thundercats; TJ Hooker; To the Manor Born; Tomorrow's World; Trap Door; Upstairs Downstairs; V; Van der Valk; The Waltons; When the Boat Comes In; Why Don't You?; Willo the Wisp; Wish You Were Here..?; WKRP in Cincinnati; Wonder Woman; Worzel Gummidge; Z Cars.

I hope that my personal recollections within this book have stirred up some warm, nostalgic memories of your own. If they have, go seek out some of your favourite programmes from the *Proper Telly* era and relive those golden days of youth. YouTube is a great place to find classics TV gems of years gone by. Watch, smile and remember that those really were the days.

ACKNOWLEDGEMENTS

I would dearly like to thank the lovely Sally Geeson for agreeing to be interviewed for my blog. Snippets of the interview have been included in this book. Many thanks also to the gentleman that is John Challis for giving me glorious insight into the magnificent Tom Selleck moustache.

Most of all, I would like to send out sincere thanks to my beautiful wife Lisa, who continually encourages me with my writing projects and gives me plenty of extra material with her own memories of life in the seventies and eighties. I couldn't do it without you Lisa.

Printed in Great Britain
by Amazon